PORTABLE FURNITURE

A PRACTICAL GUIDE TO SPACE-SAVING FURNISHINGS

by Vicki Brooks

THE MAIN STREET PRESS • Pittstown, New Jersey

For Charles, who never fails to respect my need for space.

Published by
The Main Street Press, Inc.
William Case House
Pittstown, NJ 08867

Published simultaneously in Canada by
Methuen Publications
2330 Midland Avenue
Agincourt, Ontario M1S 1P7

Printed in the United States of America

10 9 8 7 6 5 4 3 2

Cover design by Robert Reed

Text design by Frank Mahood

Library of Congress Cataloging-in-Publication Data

Brooks, Vicki.
  Portable furniture.

  Bibliography: p.
  Includes index.
  1. Furniture—Catalogs. I. Title.
TS887.B76 1986   684.1'0029'4   86-8730
ISBN 0-915590-88-3
ISBN 0-915590-87-5 (pbk.)

PORTABLE FURNITURE

Contents

INTRODUCTION
7

CHAPTER 1

Chairs
11
Folding Chairs
Stacking Chairs
Vive La Différence

CHAPTER 2

Tables
31
Folding and Knockdown Tables
Stacking and Nesting Tables
Extension/Expansion Tables
Tea Carts and Trolleys

CHAPTER 3

Beds
55
Sofa Beds and Trundle Beds
Fold-Down and Folding Beds
Futons and Low Platform Beds
Surprises

CHAPTER 4

Sofas, Love Seats, and Benches
69
Daybeds and Love Seats
Sectional and Modular Sofas
Benches

CHAPTER 5

Desks and Work Units
81
Desks
Work Units

CHAPTER 6

Shelving and Cabinets
93
Freestanding Components
Hanging Components

CHAPTER 7

Storage
111
Closet Systems and Wardrobes
Freestanding Storage Units
Hanging Racks and Utility Shelving

CHAPTER 8

Children's Furnishings
131
Beds
Storage and Accessories

CHAPTER 9

Outdoor Furniture
147
Chairs and Chaise Longues
Tables and Trolleys

CHAPTER 10

Appliances and Accessories
163
Appliances
Kitchen and Bath Accessories
Where to Hide It
Where to Hang It
The Last Word

LIST OF SUPPLIERS

179

BIBLIOGRAPHY

187

INDEX

189

Introduction

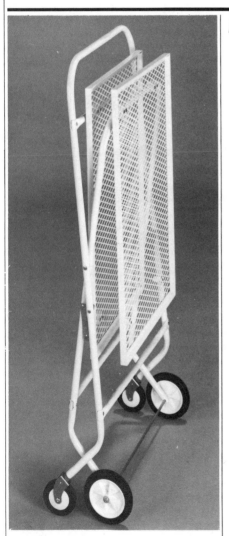

*B*etween 1975 and 1982, the average size of all new houses and apartment units built in the United States dropped from 1,526 to 1,449 square feet—a loss of over five percent of critical living space. During roughly the same period (1976 to 1984), the average cost of a new home more than doubled, from $43,340 to $89,400. And because of that increase, homeowners and tenants now devote more than thirty percent of their incomes to paying for the roofs over their heads, as opposed to roughly one quarter just ten years ago. As Joan Kron so aptly puts it in *Home-Psych*, her fascinating treatment of the psychology of home decoration, "The right to a place of your own is a luxury this country can no longer include in the gross national promise."

Because of the growing costs of shrinking space, more and more people are being forced to share living quarters not large enough for the purpose. Graduates who once would have moved away from home the minute the ink was dry on the parchment must now remain with their parents or squeeze into tiny apartments with too many roommates. Young married couples are finding it prohibitively expensive to add on or move to larger quarters as their children grow. Retirees trying to juggle fixed pensions against an ever-rising cost of

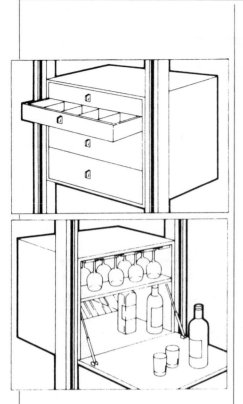

living find that their only option is to move in with their adult children, who then must tackle the thorny problem of making adequate room for them. Even those fortunate enough to have suitable housing usually find that their possessions increase with the same tenacity as outdated newspapers while their available space remains stubbornly the same.

Short of enlarging your present home, ruthlessly discarding treasured acquisitions, or finding a larger place, there is still much you can do to allieviate your space crunch, no matter what its nature. And you needn't hire a design consultant to help. If you must cope with a sardine-can kitchen, yet like to prepare gourmet meals from time to time, there are appliances and accessories scaled to fit in minimal space whose performance is up to the standards of even a master chef. If your off-season clothes and linens are crammed under the bed, a new closet system or set of modular storage pieces can transform the chaos to order. If you've recently begun to work at home and despair of ever finding a place to put your desk and papers, a folding desk and rolling file cabinet might be the answer. In short, whatever your space problem, you should find one or more potential solutions in the pages of *Portable Furniture.*

What you won't find in this book are common solutions: dime-a-dozen convertible sofas and flimsy folding chairs and tables. Each of the pieces illustrated here has been selected for inclusion on the basis of several criteria: its space-saving design, its utility, and its quality. Flexibility is paramount, whether in a folding tea cart, a coffee table that hides an extra bed, a weatherproof stacking chair, or a set of canisters that looks equally handsome placed on a counter top or hung from a rack under the kitchen cabinet.

For the sake of convenience, *Portable Furniture* is arranged by chapters according to general type of furniture, making it easy to find the subject of greatest interest to you, whether it be children's furnishings, shelving, or a sectional sofa. Yet many of the pieces are so useful and of such classic design that they could well be used in several different areas—a sleek outdoor table in the dining room, for instance, or a child's bed with trundle in the study that has to double as a guest room. So browse at your leisure; chances are you'll find a number of portable furnishings that are exactly right for your needs.

To facilitate your locating the manufacturer or retailer who carries each piece once you have made your selection, you'll find that all suppliers' names appear in bold type the first time they are mentioned in the description of a particular item. An alphabetical list of those suppliers, with their addresses, telephone numbers, and any charge for literature, begins on page 179. The index which concludes the book will guide you to all the offerings included for each supplier.

A book must be arranged with the same care and attention to space, detail, and quality as any home. To that end, I am indebted to a number of people. First, to Martin Greif, for his ideas, encouragement, and editing. To Frank Mahood, for the spaciousness and clarity of his design for text and illustrations; and to John Fox and Lisa Magaz for bringing that design to fruition. I am grateful to the many companies and entrepreneurs who made photographs and information available so willingly, and finally, to Liz Rolfe, for orchestrating with such great aplomb the reams of material they supplied.

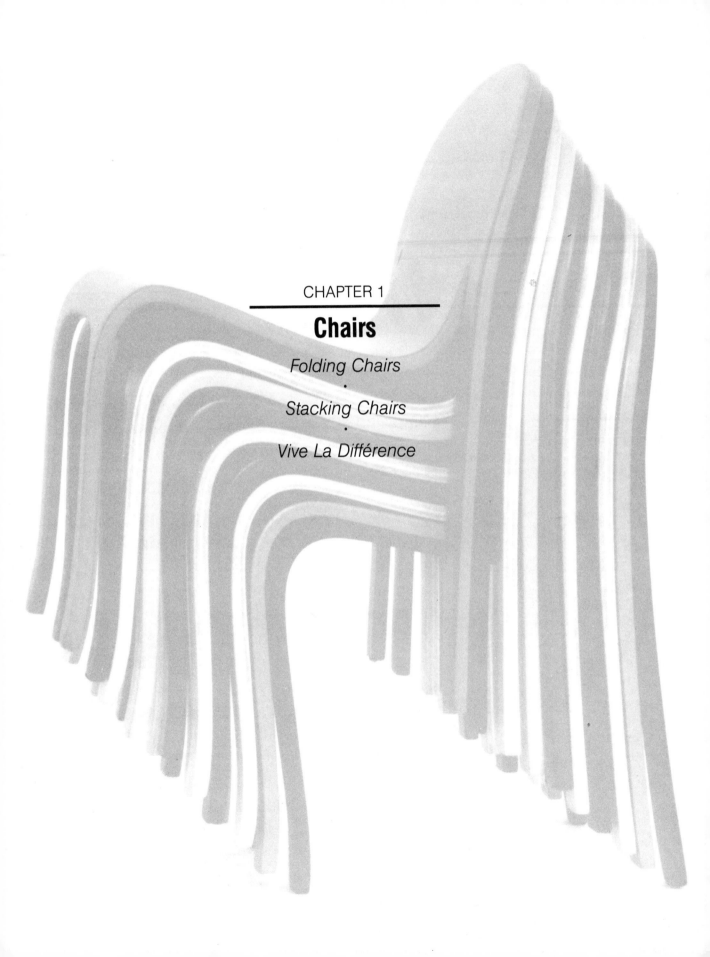

CHAPTER 1

Chairs

Folding Chairs

·

Stacking Chairs

·

Vive La Différence

Chairs

*U*ntil the sixteenth century, chairs were reserved for the nobility and the clergy; the common folk had to be content sitting on chests, benches, and stools. But, even as early as the twelfth century, portable chairs were being made. One documented example, owned by the Abbott of Glastonbury, was an armchair that was a precursor of modern knock-down furniture; it could be taken apart so that its owner could bring it with him when he traveled to less civilized areas of England. Since most early chairs were made of massive pieces of oak, however, even the "portable" ones must have been heavy and therefore difficult to lug about.

Today even the tightest budget can stretch to include a few selections from the staggering array of seating that is available. And though many of today's chairs—including recliners and some upholstered armchairs—are too large and heavy to maneuver easily, there are plenty of choices left for those to whom space, or mobility, or both, is paramount. Nor are the selections limited to oak and other hardwoods, although they are still popular materials. Handsomely designed contemporary chairs are made of aluminum and steel, and some of the most portable are molded from space-age plastics that take ingenious—yet still comfortable—

forms. Folding chairs that collapse into mere inches for storage yet have no hinges to rust or disintegrate, stacking models that can be piled to near skyscraper heights, chairs that will move from living room to patio at a whim and wear well in either location—these are just a few of the many designs offered by modern manufacturers who are sensitive to the space limitations and practical considerations faced by many of their customers.

Yet today's home furnishing companies have not neglected the past masters of good design: among the newest offerings presented in this book is a classic Marcel Breuer folding chair that was first introduced in the 1920s but whose form remains fresh and contemporary in the 1980s.

While acknowledging the timeless forms of past decades, designers and suppliers have not neglected society's current preoccupation with fitness and posture. Among the most innovative and portable of their new designs are those which force us to revise the seated position we habitually take, relieving stress on back and neck while providing the ultimate in comfort and relaxation.

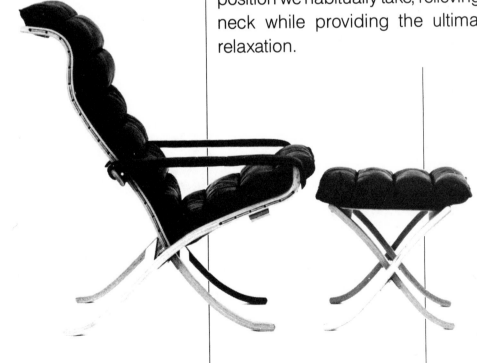

Folding Chairs

Unless you are one of the fortunate few blessed with plenty of space for entertaining, regardless of the number of friends and associates you have to accommodate, chances are that your home or apartment has a cache of folding chairs somewhere. And if you're just starting to furnish a nest for the first time, you'll probably have decided that such useful objects have to be part of your plans. But there is no need to settle for haphazardly made, badly designed wood or metal chairs, even if they only come out of the closet once or twice a year. As the examples on these pages make clear, there is a wide range of good modern design available today that will suit just about any taste and fit in almost any space. Some of the models offered are even handsome enough to hang from the wall as a form of modern sculpture when not in use.

LOCUST. It would be difficult to imagine a more useful chair than **Westnofa**'s Locust. Because it adjusts easily to any seat height from 17½ up to 29 inches (no tools required), it would serve equally well as a high stool at a kitchen counter or as extra seating at the breakfast table. Made of natural or stained beech with black or red metal support, it folds compactly for easy storage. Designer Torstein Nilsen has included an optional bracket so that it can be hung from the wall or in a closet when not needed.

WESTNOFA

Scandinavian designers are responsible for some of the most innovative home furnishings available today, and the artists who contribute their ideas to Norway's Westnofa are among the best in the field. Their concepts tend to be surprisingly simple ones, the lines of the pieces, sleek and sweeping. Natural woods are favored over man-made materials such as metal and acrylic. Many of Westnofa's offerings are designed with space limitations in mind; the firm's chairs either fold, or stack, or can be used in several different positions according to individual comfort requirements. The Locust chair shown on this page is just one example of the style and originality inherent in Westnofa furniture.

Peter W. Glasser

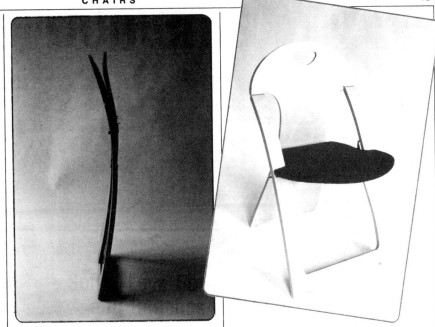

REGISTA. The ubiquitous director's chair made popular on the Hollywood movie set is certainly useful. But the standard wood-frame version with its monotone canvas seat and back has become a cliché. It's also somewhat unwieldy and hard to fold compactly. Why not try this **Pottery Barn** version instead? It features a light metal frame and two-toned canvas available in a choice of colors, and would look equally well in the living room, at the dining room table, or out in the back yard.

THE UNFOLDING CHAIR. Peter **Danko** conceived the design for this simple, two-piece molded plywood chair. In both concept and execution, it's a far cry from the flimsy wooden chairs so readily available at the local discount store. An innovative method of molding a pliable material into the chair enables it to fold without hinges. And fold it does, to a mere sliver (two inches). The seat can be padded or not, as you please.

FOLDING CHAIR. Artisan **Tom Loeser** has received wide acclaim for his furniture designs because of their sculptural qualities. Illustrated here is his folding chair, an occasional chair which collapses into a puzzle of wooden panels and stainless-steel hinges. Multi-colored pastel enamels complement the effect. Even hanging from its own rack, it is a work of art, typical of Loeser's one-of-a-kind furniture available through galleries or directly by commission.

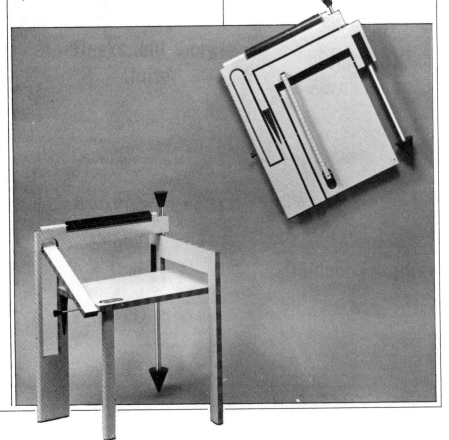

WASSILY. The club chair version of this handsome Marcel Breuer design was conceived in 1925, and is often called the Wassily because it was allegedly made for the artist Wassily Kandinsky's Bauhaus apartment. In 1926, the architect offered a folding model, also of tubular steel and fabric, but it was never produced in quantity, perhaps because the manufacturing methods of the time made the cost prohibitive. Happily, it *is* in production now, and **Palazzetti** is importing it from Italy for sale in North America. The Wassily is part of the permanent collection of The Museum of Modern Art in New York; it can now be a part of yours, as well.

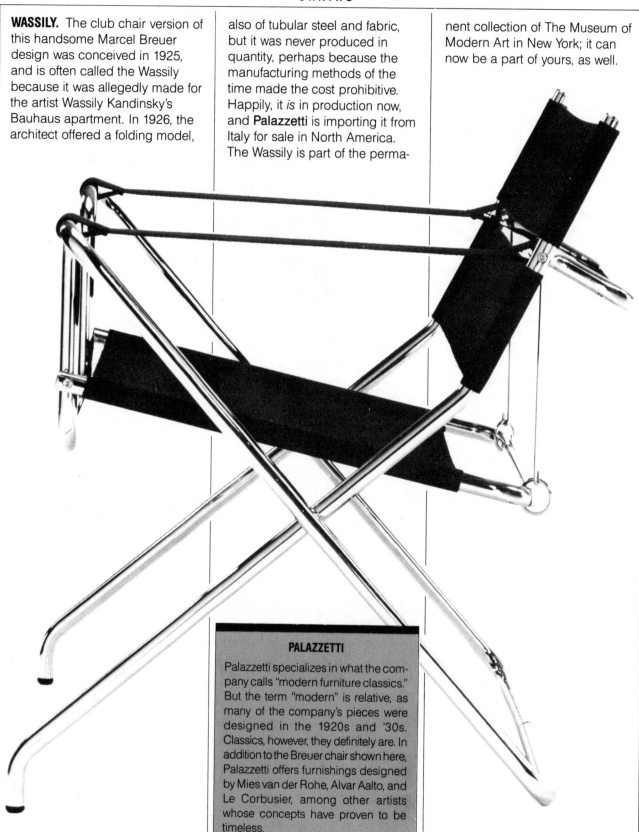

PALAZZETTI

Palazzetti specializes in what the company calls "modern furniture classics." But the term "modern" is relative, as many of the company's pieces were designed in the 1920s and '30s. Classics, however, they definitely are. In addition to the Breuer chair shown here, Palazzetti offers furnishings designed by Mies van der Rohe, Alvar Aalto, and Le Corbusier, among other artists whose concepts have proven to be timeless.

MOVIE. Interna Designs of Chicago is the American representative for a number of innovative European furniture manufacturers. Movie, made by Poltrona Frau, is composed of tubular steel finished in black epoxy. The chair seat and back are available in a wide range of leathers. The combination of man-made and natural materials results in a sleek, handsome design that would look well in most contemporary or traditional settings.

BALANS MULTI. Yes, Virginia, this *is* a folding chair! Peter Opsvik's design for **Westnofa** was derived from a revolutionary concept by H.C. Mengshoel. The higher upholstered portion is the seat; the lower, a knee rest. Your body assumes a naturally balanced position, with lower legs tucked under you, so that no undue pressure is placed on back, shoulders, and neck. The Multi, one of a number of Balans styles offered, can be adjusted to any one of four positions to provide comfortable seating for low, standard, or high desks and tables. It can be ordered in a choice of fabric colors to harmonize with any decorating scheme and is available with an optional hanger so that it can be displayed (folded flat) when not in use.

711 FOLDING CHAIR. Michael Kirkpatrick designed this handsome, sturdy chair for **CI Designs.** A simple mechanism in the hinge locks the chair in place when the seat is lowered; when it's raised, the back folds up for flat (2¼ inch) storage. Made of clear ash, the chair can be ordered with a natural cane seat or with an upholstered seat of wool homespun in deep red, terra cotta, beige, green, or dark blue.

ETOILE. Aptly named Etoile (French for "star") features an oval tubular steel frame with a starburst pattern punched into the seat. (If you're not a budding astronomer, you can have the seat in wood or wicker, as well.) Designed by Anna Anselmi, the chair can be finished in your choice of colors, including yellow, red, maroon, and green, or in more conservative white, black, or gray. Etoile is available from **Furniture of the Twentieth Century** and **Bieffe U.S.A.** Anselmi's matching Etoile table (see page 16) comes in the same range of colors and takes almost as little space to store.

FLEX. Westnofa's Flex chair folds for convenient storage when it's not needed, so you could keep it in the closet until the company arrives. But why would you want to? Ingmar Relling's design is such a handsome one that the Flex deserves pride of place opposite the sofa or near the hearth. Should you need to make room, however, Flex is even handsome when folded. A matching ottoman (not shown) is also available, and the chair back adjusts to three positions for the ultimate in comfort.

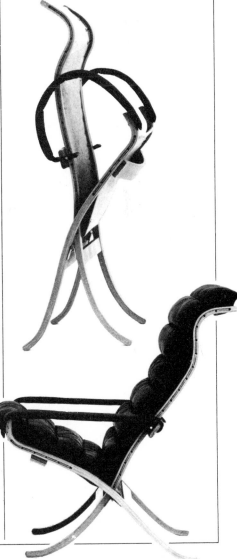

PRIMA. One of the benefits of acrylic furniture is that it will blend with any color scheme, so those extra seats around the dining table on Thanksgiving Day won't clash with the centerpiece or the tablecloth. Another benefit is its ease of maintenance (just use a damp cloth and a mild detergent when necessary). The craftsmen at **Akko** make their folding chair entirely of acrylic, so that it will be equally at ease indoors or out and won't be ruined by a sudden thun-derstorm. The Prima is available in two styles—with a clear frame with matching clear seat and back, as shown, or with the clear frame and a black seat and matching back. Or choose the back in white or red for contrast. Each Akko chair is individually numbered and surprisingly sturdy (tests prove it will support up to 450 pounds of weight).

Stacking Chairs

While there is no doubt that folding chairs are probably the optimum choice for extra seating if you have a minuscule amount of space in which to store them after visitors go home, stacking chairs, by their very nature, will prove a better investment in the long run. Because of their solid construction and lack of hardware (no hinges required), stacking chairs are sturdier. If rambunctious young children or teenagers are a part of your household, you'll find that, on average, this type of chair will last far longer and will take far more abuse than will its folding cousin. (Even the tiniest infant has a habit of becoming a clumsy adolescent almost before you know it.) As your needs change (and your square footage increases), most stacking chairs can make the transition with grace, becoming permanent seating in the new dining room or in the den, but retaining their flexibility when you need to pile them out of the way for the annual open house.

NORMAN CHERNER. The sinuous lines and sleek finish of Norman Cherner's laminated plywood armchair give it a sybaritic, romantic look. But at the same time, this classic 1954 chair is an eminently practical solution when extra seating is needed. The chair is lightweight, so it can be moved easily to any location desired. (You might even carry a few out to the patio for a fresh-air fete, as long as you remember to bring them in before it rains.) Best of all, it can be stacked when not in use. The Cherner armchair is available from **Fifty/50,** which specializes in mid-century decorative arts.

404 STACKING CHAIR. This dramatically styled side chair was designed in 1930 by Robert Mallet-Stevens, who first used it in the kitchen of a French villa. Although the slender minimal design makes it appear delicate, the Mallet-Stevens chair is, in fact, sturdy enough to be suitable in any area which gets heavy use, since it's composed of steel tubing and sheet steel. Finished in any one of a variety of electric epoxy colors, it would add a bright note whenever extra seating is required. It is available from **Palazzetti** and **Furniture of the Twentieth Century.**

PETER DANKO & ASSOCIATES

Designer Peter Danko writes: "My years as a craftsman have given me a strong respect for the qualities of wood and other materials. My designs reflect, in their functionalism, the forms and shapes I find beautiful in nature. Moreover, I strive for a visual tension, either static or kinetic, to give each piece life." Danko attains a purity of design in which each element is necessary or complements what is necessary. His resulting pieces are superb examples of what modern decorative arts should and can be.

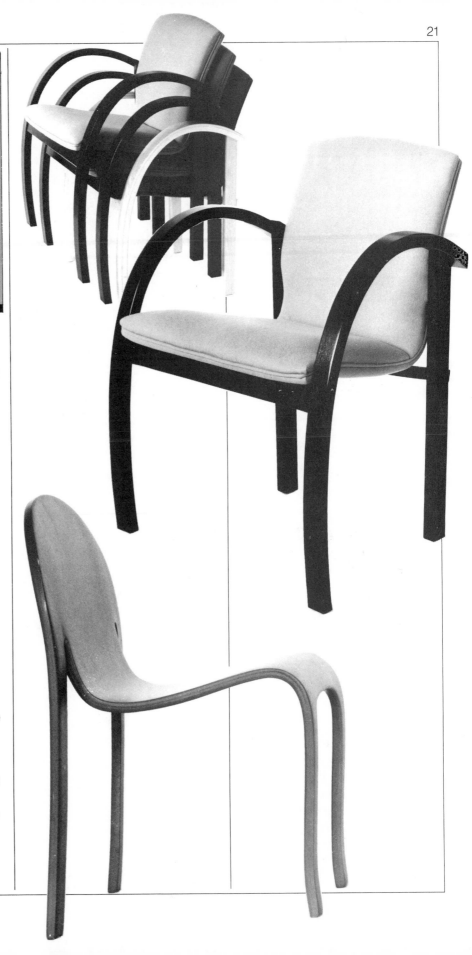

MARVIN'S CHAIR. Peter Danko's stacking armchair is made of solid beech in a natural finish. (As with all of Danko's designs, you can choose to have the frame stained a mahogany color or painted with black epoxy if you are so inclined.) Seat and back are foam-cushioned for comfort, making this a chair equally well suited for living room or dining room, no matter the number of courses or the length of the postprandial conversation.

THE BODYFORM CHAIR. Peter Danko makes this sleek beauty from one piece of molded plywood contoured to fit the natural lines of the body. Available with or without a foam seat cushion, it will stack to an indefinite height, as the photo on page 11 makes clear. Constructed of solid beech, the Bodyform chair is 30 inches high, 22 inches in depth, and 20½ inches wide, making it a suitable choice no matter how limited the space around your dining table may be.

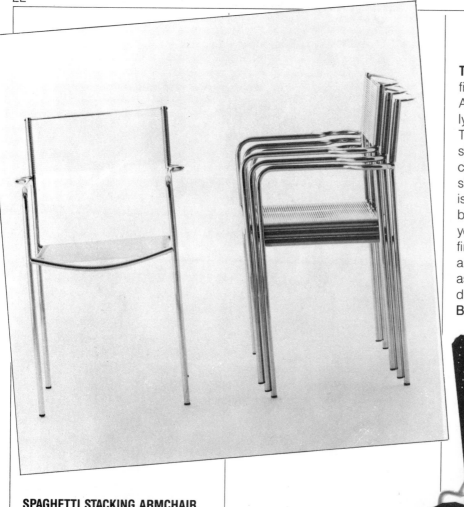

TUX. The Haigh Space design firm won a coveted Progressive Architectural award for Tux recently, and it's not hard to see why. The seat and back are of sheet steel (perforated or not, as you choose). They are attached to a slender tubular metal frame finished in neutral gray; seat and back colors are aqua, white, yellow, red, or black. Tux can be finished to withstand outdoor use and it stacks easily indoors or out, as do the matching armchair and dining table, all available from **Bieffe U.S.A.**

SPAGHETTI STACKING ARMCHAIR. Part of the Spaghetti Group designed by Giandomenico Belotti between 1960 and 1982, this ultramodern chair takes its name from the polyvinyl stringing which forms its seat and back. The frame is constructed of steel tubing which can be chromium plated or finished in baked epoxy in a choice of red, white, blue, or black; the polyvinyl stringing is available in the same colors. Matching pieces in the group include stools, dining tables, and occasional tables. If you prefer a different sort of "pasta", **International Contract Furnishings** offers the same chair frames finished with Lasagna seats and backs—that is, foam sheets held taut with steel springs.

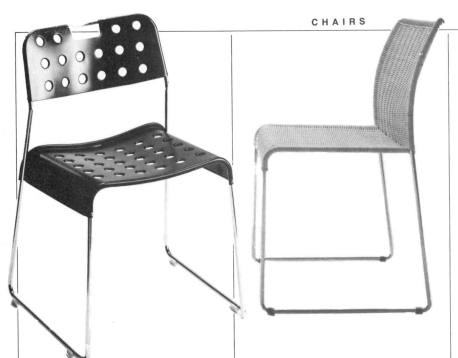

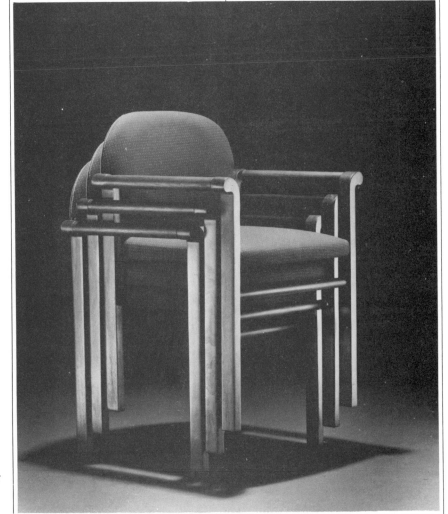

S21 STACK CHAIR. Pierantonio Bonacina of Italy manufactures this rattan and metal side chair for **MDI**, artfully wedding nature's materials with man's. The frame is available in a chrome finish or lacquered in white, black, red, green, yellow, or gray. The rattan-core seat and back are left natural, of course. MDI will supply a special trolley that can accommodate a high stack of the chairs, and offers a matching lounge for sprawling (it also can be stacked to save space).

OMKSTACK. Rodney Kinsman conceived his High-Tech design for the Omkstack chair to be manufactured in boldly perforated sheet steel with a chromium finish. Available from **Furniture of the Twentieth Century** and **Bieffe U.S.A.**, it can be ordered with its own stacking cart (on casters, of course) so that a practically unlimited number can be stored when not in use.

ION STACK CHAIR. Designed by Norman Cherner, the Ion armchair has slim, rectangular wooden legs which curve into rolled edges at the arms. **Modern Mode** offers the Ion in a choice of cherry, walnut, mahogany, or maple and in a variety of oil and lacquer finishes. Comfortable upholstery pads the seat and low back; yet even so, you can still stack half a dozen in one pile after the company goes home.

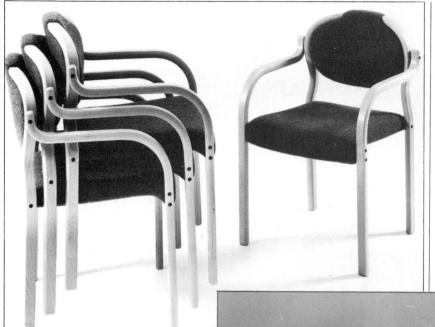

LAMINOVA. Designed by Sven Ivar Dysthe for **Westnofa**, this eye-catching armchair is made using state-of-the-art methods of lamination. The gracefully curved frame is offered in teak, walnut, rosewood, dark brown, green, red, blue, black, or natural finish. The seat and back cushions are individually molded for comfort and can be ordered in your choice of decorator colors to match or complement the wood finish chosen.

PARCO. Hartmut Elberfeld designed this rounded beech side chair and armchair to be interstacked, an unusually practical feature. **Lübke** offers Parco in a breathtaking choice of eleven different versions, including chairs with curved back stretchers, partially or fully upholstered backs, and interchangeable upholstered parts in a wide range of colors which can move from one model to another with ease. The choice of finishes for the beech frame is virtually unlimited, from any number of wood stains to a rainbow of matte lacquer colors.

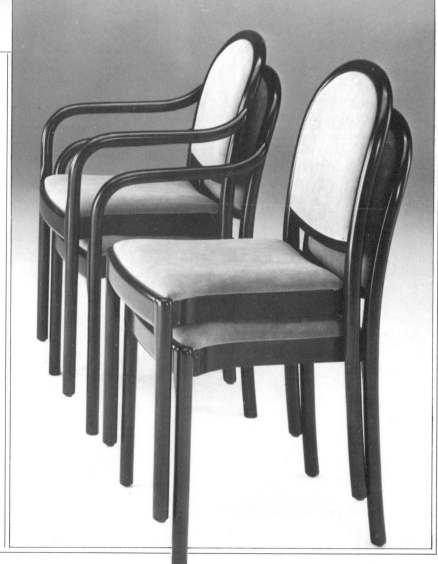

THONET

Founded in 1830, Thonet has been manufacturing fine home furnishings for more than 150 years. From its factories in North Carolina and Pennsylvania, Thonet now supplies a wide range of contemporary furniture for just about every need, whether that need includes a desk for the fledgling company office you are setting up at home, or additional wardrobe space for a burgeoning family. No matter its purpose, you can be assured that each piece will be both well designed and well constructed.

INTERLOCK STACK CHAIR. A sweep of oval steel forms the frame of Warren Snodgrass's design for **Thonet.** Its one-piece upholstered seat and back unit echoes the curves of the frame, which is available chrome-plated, brass-plated, or in beige, white, gray, or red. You can have the arms upholstered or not, as you like. Either way, Interlock stacks five high without support.

KNEKT. The clean, spare lines of the solid-beech armchair above insure that it would look well in a wide variety of settings, blending with ultramodern or traditional furnishings with equal ease. Designed by Olav Rolv Tysnes, it is offered by **Westnofa** in either natural or stained beech and in upholstery colors to suit the most demanding home decorator. Half a dozen Knekts can be stacked in one pile; the resulting area displaced will only be 33 inches wide by 44 inches high.

SOF-TECH. Designed for **Thonet** by David Rowland, the Sof-Tech collection includes both a side chair and an armchair, either of which will stack ten high without support. The unusual look of the chair derives from its vinyl-coated springs, which form both back and seat; the springs "give" with body weight and contours and thus provide both support and comfort. The frame is tubular steel, which can be finished in polished chrome plating, brass plating, or painted white, beige, gray, or red. The seat and back are available in a choice of six colors.

SKANDIA STACKING CHAIRS. Oak veneer molded plywood forms the clean, crisp lines of this **Thonet** armchair (right), designed for the company by Rud Thygesen and Johnny Sorensen. The foam-cushioned seat and back are available in a choice of colors; a side chair provides a second option. You can stack half a dozen of either model without fear that they will collapse.

IBEX. These tough yet comfortable stacking side chairs have backs of injection-molded polypropylene to match their steel frames (available in either brown or white). The upholstered seats are offered in a wide range of fabrics to match or complement the frames. No matter the color combination you choose, the Ibex will provide extra seating without taking up a lot of room; the chair measures only 20 inches in width by 19½ inches in depth and stands a mere 30 inches tall. **Arconas** manufactures this steel-framed side chair under license from Hille International.

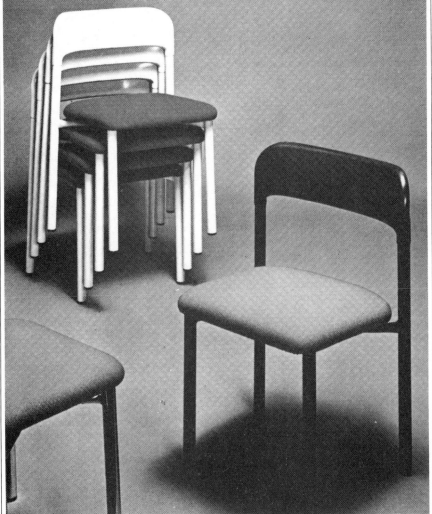

JOINT. If you're a fan of ultramodern styling, you'll certainly want to consider this sleek stacking chair from **Interna Designs**. Available with or without minimal arms, it has a no-nonsense metal frame (available in chrome-plating or blackest black); the seat and back are of black-painted wood. Joint would complement the most avant-garde High-Tech decorating scheme perfectly, either as a permanent addition to a room, or just when needed for extra seating. Both side chair and armchair measure 31½ inches high, 22 inches wide, and 17½ inches deep.

CREEK. Sottsass Associates is an Italian firm which specializes in contemporary graphic and industrial design and architecture. Its founder, Ettore Sottsass, has been a prime force in the Memphis Group, a loose affiliation of American and European designers who are creating some of the most avant-garde home furnishings available today. Creek, one of Sottsass Associates' latest efforts, is a tubular steel and polypropylene stacking side chair available from **Furniture of the Twentieth Century** and **Bieffe** U.S.A. The color combinations available are typical of ultramodern Italian design: the steel frame is painted gray, while the plastic seat and back are offered in matching gray, or in white, black, yellow, or red.

STACKING CHAIR. Curtis Erpelding's prototype for this handsome wooden side chair was an unusual three-legged version. The current model, with a leg added, is just as attractive and, like its predecessor, knocks down for shipping. The chair is made entirely of bent-laminated wood (in a choice of domestic hardwoods) and with a leather, vinyl, or fabric seat. The materials used are very light (each chair weighs only seven pounds), yet strong enough to withstand daily use, even by exuberant children.

TL20 STACK CHAIR. Thomas Lamb's design for **Nienkämper** features a steel rod frame, chrome-plated or coated, and an artfully curved laminated plywood seat and back. The one-piece plywood unit can be stained or coated with a clear finish; or you might elect to have it upholstered for added comfort.

APTA. The supreme comfort of the Apta stacking chair lies in an ingenious mechanism that adapts it to the physique of the person sitting in it, whether that person weighs 90 pounds or several hundred more. The mechanism adjusts both seats and back automatically as you sit down, and sets the most comfortable position. When *you* shift, *it* shifts. **Castelli Furniture** deals primarily with large institutional clients who need seating for many hundreds of people, but its Apta would adapt well to home use, either for seating guests in comfort during a multi-course dinner, or cradling an avid sports fan during all four quarters of the Superbowl.

Vive La Différence

If circumstances dictate that you must live in a claustrophobic studio apartment or a tiny row house with doll-sized rooms, you might think it impractical to include a comfortable lounge chair in your furnishing plans. (The ubiquitous padded recliner, which conjures up images of good book, slippers, and faithful dog, tends to be a heavy piece of furniture, not easily moved when it's time to make up the sofa bed at the end of the day.) But your choice of seating need not be limited to standard folding or stacking chairs, no matter how handsome and utilitarian they may be. Contemporary designers are full of revolutionary new ideas for seating, ideas which may make you change your thinking about what comfort really is. Two of the more unusual are shown on this page.

BOULOUM. Designed by Olivier Mourgue in 1969, the playful yet practical Bouloum richly deserves its place in the permanent collection of the Museum of Modern Art. The stacking lounge chair is shaped in the form of a human figure; its frame is composed of steel tubing comfortably upholstered in a choice of 29 colors which range from conservative gray to eye-popping purple. For outdoor use, **Arconas** will finish the Bouloum in a gel coat that is impervious to the weather.

FRONTAL 1. Most chairs are not really designed with health and comfort in mind. On the contrary, the seated position we generally assume puts extra stress on back and neck and does nothing for the circulation. **Westnofa**'s Frontal, designed by Tone Grimsrud, is guaranteed to be comfortable either for sprawling or for sitting. With the neck rest removed, its quilted base can be used alone as a stool or footstool, or can be inverted for use as a low rocking chair.

CHAPTER 2

Tables

*Folding and Knockdown
Tables*

·

*Stacking and Nesting
Tables*

·

*Extensions/Expansion
Tables*

·

Tea Carts and Trolleys

Tables

Reduced to its lowest common denominator, the basic requirement for a table is a flat, horizontal surface, raised some distance off the floor, on which to put things. The "things", ranging from place settings for twelve to frozen dinners for two and from treasured antique collectibles to a microwave oven, dictate the minimum size and height that a particular table should be to accommodate them. Whether you are just beginning to furnish your first home, or have decided to completely redecorate your present one, you'll need different tables to serve different functions. Yet selecting one table for each of its potential uses, no matter how infrequent, can severely cramp your style—and your living space. For example, it's all very well to have a massive oak refectory table in a formal, capacious dining room, but it would look odd, and be highly impractical, on permanent display in a one-room apartment (unless you plan to sleep on it as well as eat off it). By the same token, you may want to prove your hospitality by offering each of your guests a small cocktail table to rest drinks and hors d'oeuvres upon, yet on the more frequent occasions when you're not entertaining, such a thoughtful accoutrement can really limit your maneuvering room.

Fortunately, contemporary furniture designers have taken such problems into account and have solved them in interesting and innovative ways. Many of their creations, whether made of wood, metal, the newest polymers, or a combination of several materials, are inordinately practical and space-saving pieces of furniture. Some fold compactly for storage until you need them (ore particularly ingenious gate-leg table even hides four folding chairs when closed). Others can be expanded at will simply by inserting leaves or raising hinged flaps. Still others stack or nest, taking up little room as a set, but offering flexible, readily available solutions when extra table space is required.

Wheels or casters make the tea cart or trolley an especially mobile type of table—and not just for displaying the tea service. Now there are carts made specifically for the heavier objects which have become basic to modern living—television sets, microwave ovens, and food processors among them—that roll such objects effortlessly from one location to another whenever necessary. Other trolleys are designed to accommodate lighter, though no less useful, objects: they will keep towels and sundries readily at hand in the bath or guest room, for instance, or make it easy to indulge yourself with a lazy breakfast by rolling the coffeepot and plate of croissants right up to the bed.

Folding and Knockdown Tables

If you love to entertain even though your cramped quarters make it a daunting prospect, you are probably in the market for some type of folding table which can be whisked under the bed after the dishes have been cleared and the guests have gone home. There was a time when your only choice for accommodating dinner guests would have been a wobbly card table or two—hardly an appropriate base on which to display your best china and crystal. Happily, such ingeniously designed tables as those illustrated on the next few pages are readily available today, and any one of them is handsome enough to please even the most demanding company. Yet every one can be folded, or quickly dismantled, to store in a minimum amount of space until the next party or bridge game.

STADIO. Vico Magistretti is one of **Artemide**'s most talented and prolific designers. His Stadio table, part of Artemide's Reglar furniture collection, is manufactured using an exclusive fiberglass-reinforced polyester process which gives the collection its name. Reglar's color (choose white, green, dark brown, Chinese red, or light gray) is impregnated in the material rather than applied on the surface. It thus offers high resistance to nicks, scratches, and temperature extremes. Equally practical indoors or out, the Stadio table features legs that detach easily for storage in a minimal amount of space. It is shown here with a pair of Selene stacking chairs, also designed by Magistretti.

PLANO. Giancarlo Piretti's ingenious Plano folding tables are part of **Castelli Furniture**'s PL Foldables series. Both round and square models are designed to collapse into neat quarters for easy storage, yet will provide plenty of sturdy support when in use. They are shown with Piretti's Plia folding chair, which has attained permanent status in the Design Collection of the Museum of Modern Art.

R-LINE TRAY TABLES. A quartet of TV tables with its own stand is certainly practical; no matter how much room you have to entertain, there will always be occasions when an extra table or two would be a plus. **Quaker Industries** makes these handsome, solid-oak tables with a matching storage rack; the table surface measures a roomy 14½ by 19 inches.

FOLDING TV/SNACK TABLES. While cheap veneer or metal tray tables are available in any discount store, you won't find sturdy, well-designed models such as these quite as easily. **Akko** makes its acrylic tray tables with matching stands, each of which will store four folded tables. The weatherproof acrylic makes them ideal for use on lawn or patio, so you won't have to worry if you forget to bring them in from the rain. All of Akko's tray tables feature clear acrylic rod legs; tops can be had in matching clear acrylic or in red, white, or black.

ETOILE. The Etoile table at far left, designed by Anna Anselmi and available through **Bieffe U.S.A.** and **Furniture of the Twentieth Century**, is constructed of sheet and tubular steel finished in your choice of white, gray, yellow, red, maroon, green, or black. When not in use, it folds for easy storage, or can be hung neatly from the wall.

CUMANO. The Cumano folding table, similar in both style and material to the Etoile, was designed by Achille Castiglione for Zanotta of Italy and is imported by **Furniture of the Twentieth Century.** Of sheet steel and steel rods, it is sleekly finished in red, dark green, dark blue, or black.

EARTHQUAKE. Tom Loeser's high-spirited design is a contemporary work of art. Composed of fine woods (satinwood and ash are often employed), the Earthquake table is finished in enamels; by varying the colors and shapes used, Loeser insures that each table he completes will be unique. As a bonus, he puts the tables together with threaded rods running through the legs, making them easy to detach for storage.

FOLDING GATELEG TABLE. The infinitely practical gate-leg table is a boon to anyone for whom space is at a premium. As interpreted by **The Pottery Barn**, it is constructed of clear lacquer-coated hardwood that is resistant to stain and never needs polishing. When fully open, it will seat six in comfort, yet it folds to a mere 10 inches in width.

THE POTTERY BARN

The Pottery Barn has achieved deserved popularity with thousands looking for home furnishings that are well designed, durable, and reasonably priced. Many of the chairs and tables featured by the company are designed to ship and store flat, but can be assembled in just minutes using ordinary household tools. For jobs requiring more complex assembly, the firm offers on-the-spot help; for example, if you order a vinyl-coated steel closet system whose shelves must be shortened to fit your tiny cubicle, it can be cut to order while you wait, making your installation task much simpler.

DIRECTOR'S TABLE. If a table that folds flat for storage is the essence of practicality, how about one that folds and also adjusts to two different heights when you need it? **The Pottery Barn** director's table, made of lacquer-finished hardwood, has folding legs that slip into grooves on the underside of the tabletop to achieve either dining or coffee-table height at a moment's whim.

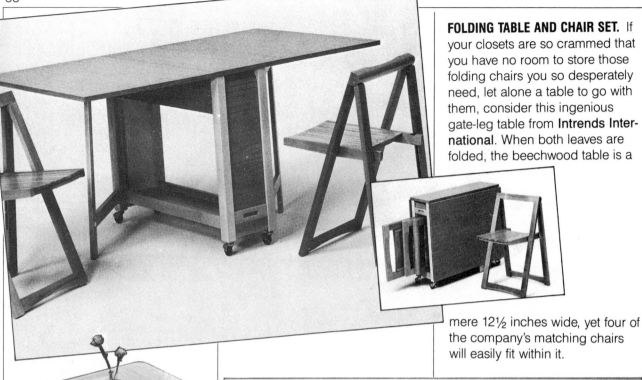

FOLDING TABLE AND CHAIR SET. If your closets are so crammed that you have no room to store those folding chairs you so desperately need, let alone a table to go with them, consider this ingenious gate-leg table from **Intrends International**. When both leaves are folded, the beechwood table is a

mere 12½ inches wide, yet four of the company's matching chairs will easily fit within it.

LYNDON COFFEE TABLE. Made of ash with beautifully crafted shiplap joining, this handsome coffee table features a square glass insert and gently rounded corners, and is finished in clear lacquer for ease of maintenance. Its three pieces simply notch together, making it easy to dismantle and slip under the sofa when you need extra room. Conceived for **Placewares** by its design subsidiary, LyndonDesign, the coffee table measures 30 inches square and is 15 inches high.

CIRCLE AND POST. Designer Michael Zevy Berkowicz combines glass, acrylic, and metal to create a table that has both classic and contemporary elements. His Circle and Post coffee table features a clear, thick glass top supported by three acrylic and metal posts. Both the posts and the caps which crown them are threaded, making them easy to unscrew when you need to dismantle the table. (Caps are available in chrome, brass, or acrylic.) If you prefer a more angular design, **Plexability** offers a four-legged square or rectangular version as well. Each is available in custom dimensions to fit your requirements.

TED. If you want to add a note of cheerful color and some much-needed counter space at the same time, why not try **Ikea**'s drop-leaf wall table? Designed by Niels Gammelgaard, the Ted table is made of epoxy-lacquered steel finished in bright red, electric blue, or sunny yellow (it's also available in black and white). The Ted folds flat against the wall when you don't need it, but, when you do, it measures a roomy 23½ by 17½ inches. Ikea also provides matching folding chairs and TV tables in the Ted series.

OMEGA. The original Omega table, designed by Hans Eichenberger in 1955, was selected for the permanent collection of the Museum of Modern Art in 1958. Since that time, Eichenberger's original concept has grown to include many models—desks, conference tables, and credenzas among

them—interpreted in both woods and man-made materials. **Stendig** offers the Omega folding table in two sizes: 33 by 72 inches and 33 by 78 inches. Both are available in the standard dining and work height (28½ inches). The top is white plastic laminate; the base, steel tubing with a shining chrome finish.

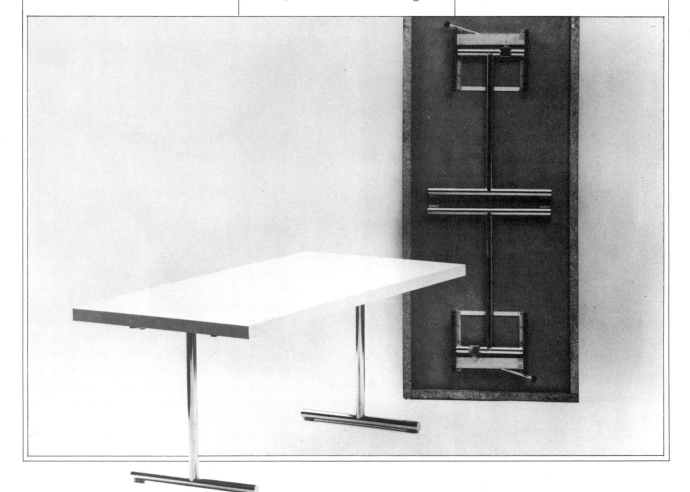

Stacking and Nesting Tables

Stacking or nesting tables offer unusual flexibility in just about any room setting. A trio of nested tables takes up little space, yet provides extra room for cocktail glasses or buffet dinner plates at a moment's notice. If you purchase such a set for a tiny studio apartment, they will be equally useful when you move into your first house or a roomier apartment. Carefully chosen for style and durability, they can go from living room to bedroom or den with great aplomb and will still be available to pull out if needed for special functions. Several of the models featured in this section can move inside or out with equal ease, as they are composed of modern materials that remain impervious to cold or damp; others are modular units that will look well whether butted together for maximum tabletop space or used as single pieces beside separate chairs.

Z TABLES. From Xylem, his studio in Seattle, **René Soulard** creates handsome wood furnishings that reflect his respect for natural materials. His aptly named Z tables are not only useful pieces of furniture, but also strong sculptural compositions. Pushed together, they can serve as a coffee table (each stands 18 inches high); separated, they are excellent end or cocktail tables. Soulard uses the same dramatic "Z" design for dining room tables and chairs; you might like to have a matched set.

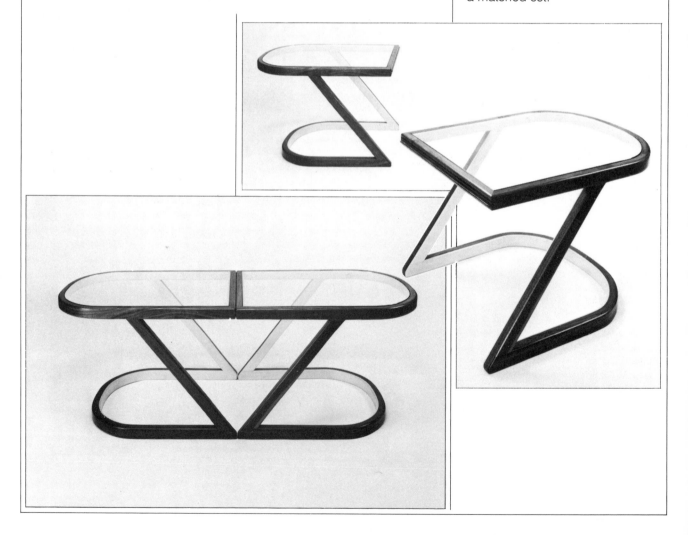

SCARTHIN NICK. Ronald Carter's trio of nesting tables was designed for Britain's Peter Miles Furniture and is imported by **Interna Designs.** The spare, angular lines of the pieces would blend well with many furniture styles. Composed of ash, the tables feature glass tops for easy maintenance, but can be built of solid hardwoods if you prefer. The largest table measures roughly 36 inches long and 16 inches wide and stands 19 inches tall. The twins beneath it are 16¼ inches square and 16 inches tall.

WATERFALL WIDE-BEND. It would be easy to imagine many occasions when this trio of clear acrylic nesting tables could be useful. When you realize that they double as benches, and that **Akko** supplies comfortable cushions for them, they become even more practical. Akko offers the same sweeping design with casters added for greater mobility. The largest table shown is 17 inches high and nearly 20 inches wide; the smallest, 15 inches high and 16½ inches wide. Cushions are offered in a number of fabrics, including weatherproof vinyl, or you can supply your own material.

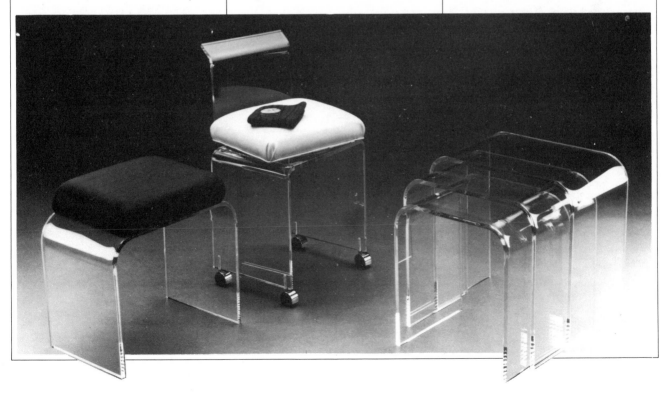

LILY PAD TABLES. Michael Zevy Berkowicz's quartet of glass and acrylic tables features green-tinted glass tops and heavily beveled acrylic bases. They can be grouped together, as shown, to create an interesting multi-level table (the whole, 27 inches in diameter), or used separately or in smaller groupings. **Plexability** offers custom sizes to suit your requirements.

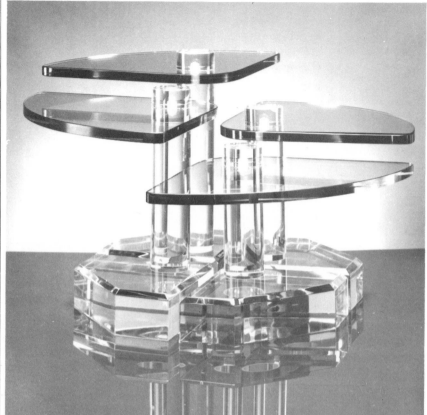

TRIANGULAR TABLES. Liza Lamb puts her handmade fabrics to a number of uses, such as attaching them to screen panels and to paneled tables like these. The tops are glass, and the panels are 24 inches high and 18 inches wide; a pair of her tables would serve equally well flanking a sofa or placed together at one end for a squared-off effect. Lamb will custom match her cotton fabrics with the interiors of her clients' homes on special request.

LIZA LAMB

Liza Lamb's furniture incorporates her beginnings as a weaver with a later interest in lacquered wood forms. The blending of her handwoven cottons and angular pieces works extremely well, since Lamb's textile designs tend to the geometric and their patterns often mirror the shapes of the furniture pieces. Among the items Lamb commonly makes available are several occasional tables and a handsome wood and fabric screen. She frequently takes on special commissions, working with architects and designers to create custom pieces for contemporary interiors.

NESTING TABLES. Sheet steel laminated in a wide choice of colors (including bold blues, reds, and yellows) is molded to form this set of nesting tables for **Amisco.** The largest of the three is 17½ inches tall and 22 inches wide; the smallest, 14½ inches by 16 inches. The company offers a variety of laminated steel tables to mix or match with its nesting set: trolleys, coffee tables, and bedside tables are just a few of the choices.

DEMETRIO. Part of **Artemide**'s Reglar collection of fiberglass-reinforced polyester furniture, Demetrio was designed by Vico Magistretti as a sleek, minimally styled low side table that can be stacked in innumerable ways to form a higher table or étagère. Artemide makes both the side table and Magistretti's larger occasional table (not shown) in white, green, dark brown, Chinese red, and light gray. (You might want to combine several colors for an interesting effect).

Extension/Expansion Tables

As the average square footage of new houses and apartments has shrunk in recent years, so, too, has the amount of space devoted to dining rooms and breakfast nooks. As a consequence, formal dinners for more than four people or so have become difficult to engineer. A buffet supper, with its attendant plate and glass juggling, is one solution. It is possible, however, to choose a compact table that will seat at least two people comfortably during normal use, yet provide the flexibility of expanding to double or triple size for special occasions. Most of the extending tables shown on these pages are small enough when closed to keep against a wall where they won't impede traffic flow, but can be pulled out and enlarged to accommodate a sizeable group at a moment's notice. So invite the crowd with impunity, take the folding chairs out of the closet, and enjoy the feast.

KOTZIAN DINING TABLE. Designer Henry Kotzian created this unusual circular extension table. When the eight pie-shaped sections are moved apart (they are affixed to a track, so a slight turn of the table separates them), eight arrow-shaped leaves can be inserted to double seating from six to twelve. The table's diameter without leaves is 60 inches; with leaves, 84 inches. **Greenbaum** makes the table available in a number of luxurious woods.

FLIP FLOP TABLE. Whether you choose **General Mica Corporation**'s Flip Flop Table (*right* and *above*) in a 30-inch square size or in the larger 36- or 42-inch versions, at the flick of a wrist you can have a surface exactly double the length of the original anytime you need it. (All three models are a standard 29 inches high, and come with 2¼- or 3-inch square legs.) No matter which model you select, General Mica will provide a wide color choice of decorative laminate finishes.

DROP-LEAF PEDESTAL TABLE. Composed of Brazilian hardwood finished in clear lacquer to retard stains and grime, this space-saving round table from **The Pottery Barn** will seat four for brunch, supper, or cards (when open, it's 36 inches in diameter). But the leaves fold so that it can be easily placed against the wall, out of the traffic flow. Because it is still a fairly generous 20 inches wide when folded, it could provide extra counter space in kitchen or dining area, or display favorite collectibles in living room or hallway.

DOUBLE PEDESTAL EXTENSION TABLE. The thick glass top of **Vladimir Kagan**'s classic extension table is supported by two pedestals and heavy-duty satin aluminum extrusions. Using pull-out supports concealed in the extrusions, a pair of 24-inch leaves (available in natural woods or lacquers) can be locked into the ends. Both pedestals have built-in leveling guides, insuring a stable surface for your best china and crystal to rest upon.

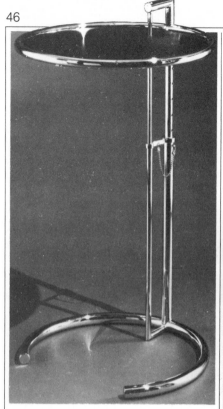

EILEEN GRAY TABLE. This classic bedside table was designed by Eileen Gray for her own home on the French Riviera during the 1920s. The smoked-glass top can be raised or lowered on its tubular steel frame using a simple locking mechanism (maximum height is 36½ inches). The Gray table is represented in the **Museum of Modern Art**'s Design Collection and is available through the Museum and from **Palazzetti**.

TEAK TABLE. Teak is among the most handsome and mellow of woods, appropriate for any number of home furnishings. **Scandinavian Design** uses it to form a classic, functional dinner table finished with teak edging and solid-brass hardware. As the two illustrations below show, it would make an attractive sideboard or hall table when closed. Yet, simply by extending the top, it becomes a roomy dining table (expanding from 20 to 40 inches in width). Static dimensions are its length (63 inches) and height (28 inches).

KORPI. Ikea's Korpi drop-leaf table is made of solid spruce finished with a clear lacquer to retard stains and provide easy maintenance. With the leaf extended, it measures 66¾ inches in length; closed, it is 47½ inches long. Korpi is just one of several practical drop-leaf tables Ikea can provide. Each is available with matching chairs and buffets; some of the tables can be ordered with an extra detachable leaf for even greater flexibility.

BUTTERFLY DROP-LEAF. When its gently rounded drop leaves are extended, this handsome oak table measures a generous 68 by 42 inches. (larger sizes are available). When both leaves are closed, the table top is reduced to 26 inches in width. **Strictly Coun-** try will finish the wood in a light, medium, or dark oak stain to suit your taste, or will craft it of cherry, if you prefer. The company also offers a rectangular version of this eighteenth-century style, which it calls the Harvest model.

WITNEY DROP-LEAF TABLE. The standard version of this solid-ash dining table (*right*) will seat up to eight people, but **Interna Designs** will import it in any size to meet your requirements. Designed by Ronald Carter for Peter Miles Furniture, it is composed of a planked three-piece top resting on two solid ends. The leaves are hinged with brass. When both leaves are dropped, the table is only 22 inches wide; with leaves extended, a roomy 70 inches.

MACKINTOSH DINING TABLE. Charles Rennie Mackintosh (1868-1928) was a Scottish designer and architect closely identified with the Constructionist and Art Nouveau schools. While his designs have inspired many other artists in the years since his death, his mastery of geometric forms remains his own. **Atelier International,** under license from the Mackintosh estate, has reproduced a variety of his tables and chairs, including an oval drop-leaf dining table (shown here with a pair of Mackintosh armchairs), which measures nearly 70 inches in width when extended. It is made of solid hardwoods with mortise and tenon construction and is finished with black ebony stain.

Tea Carts and Trolleys

While tea carts and trolleys are not essential pieces of furniture, they are certainly utilitarian ones, whether used indoors or out. Casters or wheels make it easy to roll them out of the way when not needed, but many of the current designs are handsome enough to be on permanent display in a living or dining room. Some have removable shelves which can do double duty as trays; others fold compactly so that they can be stored until needed. Contemporary uses are practically unlimited: special models are designed as "entertainment centers," with shelves specifically made to accommodate the television set, the VCR, and even the stereo system. Other trolleys, intended for use in bedroom or bath, serve as moveable storage pieces for towels, sundries, and even clothes. And still others are fitted with butcher-block tops, adding much-needed counter space to a tiny kitchen, while providing extra storage below.

FOLDING TROLLEY. Designed by Louis Lucien Lepoix and manufactured in West Germany by FRZ-Mettallwarenfabrik, this sturdy trolley folds for storage to a width of only three inches. Self-locking handles on each side easily open and close the collapsible metal frame. Plastic-coated in white or black for easy cleaning, it is shown here with Giandomenico Belotti's Spaghetti Chair. Both pieces are from the **Museum of Modern Art**'s Design Collection.

THE MUSEUM OF MODERN ART

While good contemporary furniture design is represented in thousands of retail outlets around the world, only the best can be found in the permanent collections of the world's great museums. Happily for devotees of its collections, the Museum of Modern Art makes a number of pieces from its permanent holdings available to the public via its retail store and its catalogues. Among the artists whose extraordinary work is represented in the Museum's current offerings are Alvar Aalto, Vico Magistretti, Ettore Sottsass, Jr., Eileen Gray, and Richard Sapper.

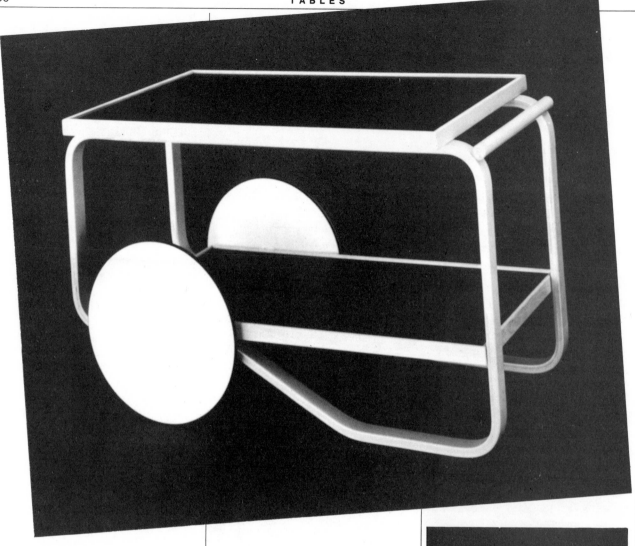

AALTO TEA CART. Alvar Aalto designed this tea cart in 1936, though its contemporary lines could have been conceived yesterday. Manufactured by Artek in Finland, it is represented in the Design Collection of the **Museum of Modern Art** and available from the Museum and from **Palazzetti.** The Aalto trolley has a frame of solid natural birch and shelves of glossy black linoleum. Twin white-lacquered wheels with rubber treads enable it to be rolled smoothly from place to place.

BUTLER. Designed by Sottsass Associates and available from **Bieffe U.S.A.,** the Butler dumbwaiter is sturdy enough to take outdoors but attractive enough to use inside as well. Equipped with casters, it rests on four thick legs available in black, gray, white, yellow, or red. The blue or black shelves are removable, as is the bottle rack. The whole is framed with chrome tubing.

HUTCH-TOP GOURMET CENTER. The open shelf of **Van Pelt**'s practical Gourmet Center is designed to accommodate a standard microwave oven; small appliances can easily be stored behind the wood-handled doors beneath it. Van Pelt offers its hutch-top model with a laminated finish (either white or simulated oak) for easy maintenance; it rests on four heavy-duty casters which make moving it a breeze. Like most of Van Pelt's furnishings, the center is shipped knocked down, but can be assembled easily using standard household tools.

MOBILE SERVICE CART. Clear acrylic and bright metal accents are featured in **Generai Mica**'s rolling trolley, one of many pieces in the company's Brenner Collection. A matching portable bar (not shown) will rest easily on the bottom shelf; the bar has a rack that accommodates ten stemmed glasses, with space for several bottles between them.

TEAK TROLLEYS. The ever-widening popularity of VCRs and home computers presents a new design challenge for furniture manufacturers: to provide specific pieces that will accommodate these high-technology wonders while retaining the overall feeling of a more traditional decorating scheme. One solution, of course, is to hide the machinery behind closed doors. But if constant use demands that the computer and the television remain readily accessible, **Scandinavian Design** offers two teak trolleys that are both handsomely styled and practical solutions.

SERVING CART. Clear acrylic is teamed with chrome-hooded casters in a sleek, modern trolley from **Akko** which measures 27 inches wide by 16 deep and a generous 35 inches high. Its three spacious shelves are an especial-ly useful feature, as is its weather-proof material, which enables you to wheel it from patio to house and back again without fear that it will be affected by rain or discolored by sun.

BATH/BOUDOIR CART. Offered in either clear or black acrylic or in a combination of the two (with clear sides and black shelves), **Akko**'s useful bath cart rolls easily on four casters. It provides three roomy shelves for towels and supplies, along with handy towel racks on either side. Only 13 inches deep and 24 inches wide, it could be stashed in a corner when not needed.

AKKO

In its factories in suburban Boston, Akko makes occasional furniture and accessories from acrylic, a medium that is not affected by light or moisture and is easy to maintain in sparkling condition with just mild soap and water. The company's offerings range from trolleys and vanities to chairs and bar stools (some available with removable cushions for extra comfort).

TEA TROLLEY. This three-shelf acrylic and glass tea trolley was designed by Michael Zevy Berkowicz of **Plexability.** Its wheels permit easy mobility; the graduated glass shelves provide ample room for food and service pieces. Plexability offers the trolley in a standard size (36 inches long by 16 inches wide and 36 high), or it can be manufactured in custom dimensions to suit your requirements.

MOBILE SERVER. Two compartments, each containing an adjustable shelf, are contained within the double doors of **Henredon**'s brass-trimmed wooden server. The top opens to a roomy 76 inches, exposing a heat- and alcohol-resistant black laminate surface. When closed, the piece measures 38 inches in width by 18 inches deep.

ELFA KITCHEN TROLLEY. This wire basket storage trolley is comprised of modular components chosen from Sweden's Elfa system. Available in North America from **Placewares** and **Lynk,** the Elfa system offers 23 frame sizes and 31 basket sizes; you can stack various components or clip them side by side in virtually endless arrangements. Topped with a maple butcher block (or a Birch or Formica top, two other options) and fitted with four casters, the model illustrated would be an immensely practical addition to a small kitchen.

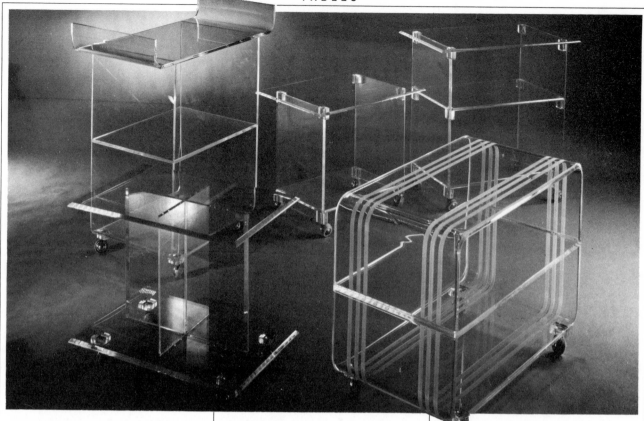

TV TABLES. Unless you still treasure that old behemoth console-model television and don't mind straining your back every time you need to move it, chances are that you have a somewhat more manageable portable set. Even so, you need a place to put it. Why not choose one of these Plexiglas trolleys from **Plexi-Craft?** Each will provide welcome additional shelf space and display the TV in style.

STRAJK. Designed by Tomas Jelinek for **Ikea,** this useful serving table is made of particle board on a chromium-plated steel frame. The particle board can be finished in pine or teak veneer or in a white lacquer coating. In addition to its roomy top and bottom shelves, it features a handy magazine rack, just the thing to hold the Sunday paper for breakfast in bed, or to keep the weekly TV listings close by a favorite easy chair. The open design of the Strajk cart permits it to be drawn close to the bed or sofa; the bottom shelf is low enough to slip under many pieces of furniture, so that the tea, or lunch, or cocktail, can be placed within easy reach.

CHAPTER 3

Beds

*Sofa Beds and Trundle
Beds*

·

*Fold-Down and Folding
Beds*

·

*Futons and Low Plat-
form Beds*

·

Surprises

Beds

*U*nless you are a hopeless insomniac, the bed you select will be the item of furniture that you use the most regularly over a period of many years. It should therefore be chosen with great care and attention, not only to its style, but to the quality of its construction and to its durability. Yet no matter how well made, a standard mattress and box spring combination is heavy and awkward to move, whether you just want to do the annual heavy cleaning or are being transferred to another town. It is also a space hog, taking up more proportional floor area than just about any other piece of furniture (with the possible exception of a treasured grand piano).

Even if you have a wonderfully roomy bedroom and can select a luxurious queen- or king-size bed to put in it, there will probably be occasions when you would like to accommodate overnight or weekend guests. But with available space generally at a premium, the living room or office at home may have to do double duty as a guest bedroom. (For ideas on how to enlarge the capacity of a child's bedroom, see Chapter 8). Fortunately, there are lots of alternatives to the standard bed, alternatives that will not only provide a good night's sleep for you or your occasional visitors but serve other useful functions after the alarm goes off in the morning.

By far the most common choice is the convertible sofa or sofa bed. This is one piece of furniture, however, that you definitely should not stint on, especially if it will be used on a daily basis. Even if you only open it up for guests once in a great while, pick one that is sturdily made and that has a firm, comfortable mattress. Cheap sofa beds may save money in the short run, but they will do nothing for your—or your guest's—back or temper. You might, instead, opt for a light, portable Japanese futon, which goes from chair to bed at the flick of a wrist. Or choose a total storage system which provides a fold-down bed plus lots of space for clothes and collectibles, though it juts out only a foot or so from the wall. Or select a well-upholstered easy chair, always a welcome addition to any living area, but even more welcome if it hides a bed that can be utilized at a moment's notice. Or pick a coffee table that does double duty as a queen-size bed. Any one of these options will allow you the regular use of a great deal of floor space that would be permanently lost with the addition of a standard bed.

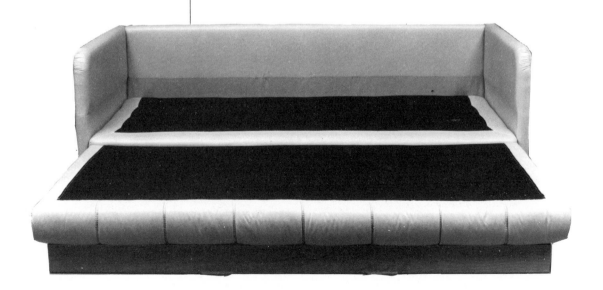

Sofa Beds and Trundle Beds

Whether you are in the market for a convertible sofa or trundle bed because your tiny living quarters can't accommodate the large brass bed you'd really like to have, or because you'd like the ability to put up an overnight guest occasionally, you'll want to give a lot of consideration to the type of piece you choose. A badly made sofa bed with lumpy upholstery and inadequate support will not wear well and is really nothing more than a thinly disguised torture chamber, even if it's only slept on once or twice a year. By the same token, a handsome, well-padded sofa bed or trundle with firm mattresses and solid construction will be a durable as well as useful addition to your living room or den. (Trundle beds designed especially for children are featured in Chapter 8.)

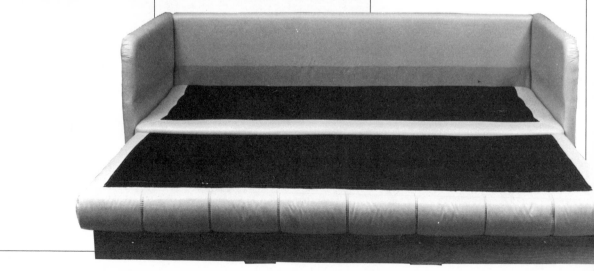

DUX INTERIORS

From its home offices in Sweden, Dux exports fine contemporary home furnishings to a New York showroom; its products are also available in many furniture stores across North America. The company's specialty is handsome, supremely comfortable beds, manufactured in various sizes with several different types of mattresses. For its beds, sofas, and chairs, Dux supplies hundreds of different upholstery and cover fabrics. In addition, the firm offers several different wall storage systems composed of a variety of functional modular units.

RIVIERA. The Riviera is a superbly designed sofa that becomes a very comfortable bed whenever you need it. It can be used as a permanent bed for one in a studio apartment, or opens up to two free-standing beds, both with inner springs beneath the thin, washable top mattresses. Available with either one or two arms, the Riviera has an optional drawer in the base to store extra bed coverings. **Dux Interiors** offers a wide choice of cover fabrics, or you can supply your own.

RIVERDALE. A generously sized sofa (87 inches in width) which opens to reveal an equally generous queen-size bed would be a practical addition to just about any living room or den. **Scandinavian Design** makes a durable, hardwood-framed sleep sofa with careful attention to detail. Joints are double-dowelled, glued, corner blocked, and carefully reinforced. A matching love seat and chair are also available, all upholstered in a choice of cotton blend fabrics.

SLEEP LOVE SEAT. Handcrafted from kiln-dried Southern yellow pine, this love seat/sleeper can be upholstered in a wide choice of fabrics. For extra comfort, you might elect to have cushioned arm caps added to cradle your elbows. The **Pine Factory** makes matching chairs, recliners, and three-cushion sofas (the sofa is also available with a hidden bed).

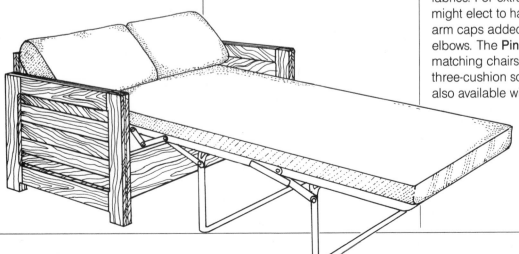

DAKOTA. Not only does the stylish Dakota sofa open to a comfortable double bed, but it has other practical features reflecting the careful thought that went into its design. The cover is made of quilted cotton and is removable for machine washing. In addition, the Dakota sports two detachable armrest cushions, each with a convenient pocket on the outside where you can stash a current book, magazine, or the daily paper. The Dakota is just one of a number of good-looking sofa beds available from **Ikea.**

WHITE LACQUERED TRUNDLE BED. The bottom section of this trundle bed, when pulled out, rises to the same height as the top section. When the bed is not needed and the top is piled high with pillows, it would make a cheerful addition to any informal setting. The **Workbench** offers its trundle bed in a white lacquered finish that is easy to maintain, or in teak or oak veneer.

AMISCO TRUNDLE. Made of steel tubing with a colorful lacquer coating, **Amisco**'s trundle bed can be ordered alone to slip under a bed or sofa you already have, or as an adjunct to the company's handsome single bed frame with gently curved head and footboards (as shown). The trundle rolls on casters, so it can be whisked out and unfolded at a moment's notice. (Mattresses are not included.)

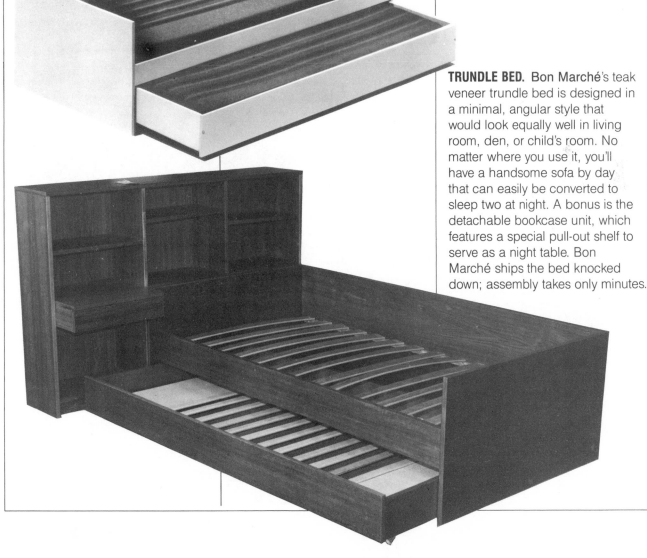

TRUNDLE BED. Bon Marché's teak veneer trundle bed is designed in a minimal, angular style that would look equally well in living room, den, or child's room. No matter where you use it, you'll have a handsome sofa by day that can easily be converted to sleep two at night. A bonus is the detachable bookcase unit, which features a special pull-out shelf to serve as a night table. Bon Marché ships the bed knocked down; assembly takes only minutes.

Fold-Down and Folding Beds

While fold-down wall beds are a boon to anyone who has to make a comfortable home from a one-room apartment, they also can be a bonus to those for whom space is not so critical. One of the side benefits of most wall-folding bed systems is their cabinetry—generally available in a choice of modular units—which can supply welcome added storage space for off-season clothing, the mushrooming book collection, the best china, and much more. And, of course, the cabinets provide durable and comfortable extra beds that are hidden from view until needed, but which can be made available at the touch of a finger. If a complete wall sleeping system is too ambitious for you but you'd still like to have an extra bed available, you can choose a compact, single folding bed that is easy to store and can be rolled out whenever you need it.

AVANTI. Offered as part of the **Dux** Avanti wall system, this fold-down bed is available in five sizes, with the practical Dux thin top mattress laid over an inner spring mattress for extra comfort. In any size, the bed is available in either a soft or firm model. The flanking wall units come in endless variations and can be tailored for any interior. Modules are offered that encompass everything from dining tables and desks to wardrobes, television sets, stereo systems, and refrigerators.

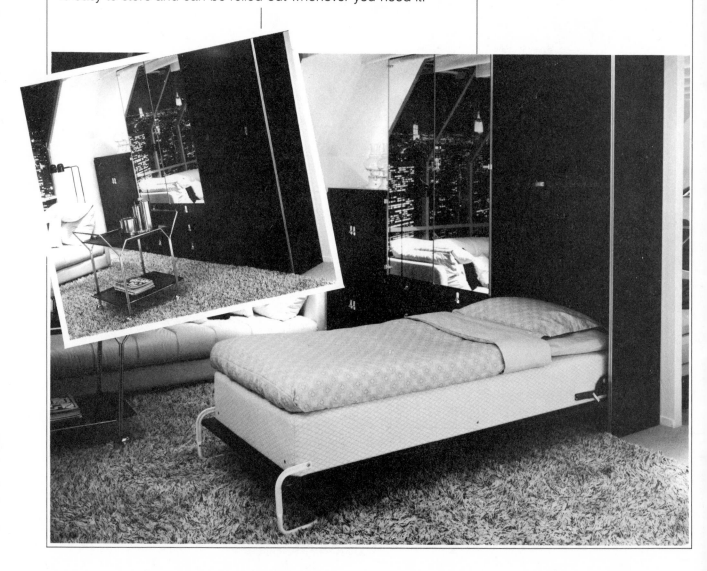

MURPHY BED. Patented counterbalance units make it easy to operate the **Murphy Door Bed Company** fold-down bed. Many models and sizes are available either with flanking cabinets or without, so that you can supply your own storage units if you like. (One of the company's newest models folds down from a sidewise, rather than a lengthwise, position—a particular boon if your room is quite narrow.) Each bed has a built-in box spring; you supply the mattress. No matter which model you choose, when folded into the cabinetry it will take only 12 or 13 inches of valuable space from the width of the room.

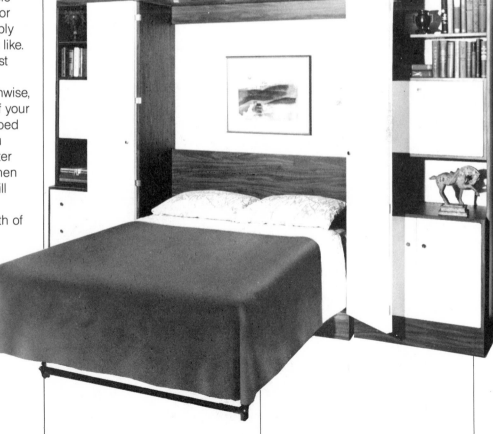

ROLL-A-WAY COT. If you are blessed with ample closet or basement space for storage and don't really need a complete wall-folding bed system, but would like the capacity to accommodate unexpected overnight guests, you might want to consider one or two of **Thonet**'s handy folding cots. Far sturdier than the usual rickety product on the market, and available in twin size only, the cots are constructed of durable steel and move easily on four swivel casters. Thonet supplies the mattress.

EUROBED. Unlike most fold-down wall beds, **Sico**'s Eurobed is supported on either side by its custom cabinets and thus does not have to be fastened to the floor. The bed pivots on vertical supports attached to the cabinets, making it effortless to maneuver; the legs fold up and over the mattress (which Sico supplies), holding it in place when it is raised. Optional accent lighting can be tucked behind the header. Sico offers seven modular wall system units to flank the bed. Whichever unit you choose, it will extend less than 19 inches from the wall when closed. Cabinets are finished in easy-to-maintain almond or oak wood-grain laminates.

Futons and Low Platform Beds

The spare, minimal lifestyle favored by the Japanese has become increasingly popular in the West; nowhere is that popularity more evident than in the use of the futon, which is now widely available in North America. Light and easy to move from place to place, it can be used as a chair, a chaise longue, or a bed. Ingenious built-in ratcheted frames allow its employment in all three ways without any additional supporting structure, but separate frames are offered that will accommodate the mattresses if you prefer to have something between you and the floor. By contrast, the platform bed is generally a large and cumbersome piece of furniture, usually composed of one or two solid hardwood forms which are difficult to maneuver. Happily, the concept of the platform bed is being reexamined by contemporary craftsmen who have retained its functional aspects while eliminating much that was awkward and unmanageable about the original.

BEDCRAFT

Rick Miller has been producing hand-made loft and platform beds since the mid-1970s. His new company, Bedcraft, specializes exclusively in the platform beds which he created with the help of noted furniture designer Peter Danko. Their careful work includes a thoughtful touch: all corners are rounded to minimize the danger of barking your shins, a hazard with the angular construction of most hardwood bed frames.

PLATFORM BED. Interlocking oak pieces fit together quickly and easily without tools to form a handsome platform bed that is easy to set up and take down whenever you like. Either left unfinished or given a final polish with oil or walnut stain, it is offered by **Bedcraft** in twin, double, queen, and king sizes. The ingenious design includes a storage section for extra blankets or seasonal items, reached by simply lifting the top. The light foam mattress is included.

DOOR STORE FUTON. White cotton duck with a red or black pencil stripe covers this twin-sized futon from the **Door Store.** A ratchet mechanism enables you to change the position of the futon quickly and easily; handy buckles keep it firmly in place when the bottom is folded underneath to form a comfortable, informal chair.

FUTON SOFA-SLEEPER. During the day, this ingenious futon combination offered by **Conran's** is a comfortable sofa with matching end tables. By night, it can be turned into a cozy double bed simply by moving the twin tables in front of the sofa frame and unfolding the two futons on top of them. The tables and sofa frame are made of solid ash with red-stained legs; each futon is stuffed with cotton batting beneath a cotton cover. The sofa measures roughly 5 feet wide by 44 inches deep; each end table is 7 inches high and about 30 inches square.

FUTON RACK. Amisco's handy futon rack can be used in either of two positions. Unfolded, its steel mesh and tubing system provides comfortable support for a light mattress while elevating it off the floor. It can also be propped up as shown, so that the futon, draped over it, makes a cozy chair. Available in three widths (40, 54, or 60 inches), it is finished in a choice of colorful laminates. Amisco also makes a fixed, L-shaped frame with its base flush to the floor. Both can be easily disassembled for storage.

THREE-WAY FUTON. A built-in ratchet frame enables **The Pottery Barn**'s futon to be switched effortlessly from a chair to a lounge or a bed as the situation requires. Its Scotch-guarded cover is made of practical cotton duck and is available in either gray or red. The Pottery Barn packs the futon in a convenient carton with a carrying handle, so you can take it along to a vacation cottage or weekend house if you are so inclined, or stow it neatly in a closet when it's not needed.

Surprises

Sofa beds remain the most popular choice among people who require extra sleeping accommodations for occasional overnight guests or who can't fit both a standard bed and a roomy couch in the tiny studio apartment they occupy. But they are by no means the only option available today. Other, smaller pieces of furniture—including chairs and coffee tables—hide comfortable beds with mattresses that range from twin size to queen. All are totally unobtrusive when closed, but can quickly be made up when the unexpected guests arrive just before "lights out." Many of them are lighter and thus more portable than the standard convertible sofa—an added attraction if you move, or even if you like to rearrange the furniture as often as you change the bed linen.

HIDE-A-BED OTTOMAN. Part of **Thonet**'s Devlin collection (which also includes an armchair and a two-cushion sofa), this comfortably padded ottoman hides an iron and steel bed mechanism which opens to provide a single (25 by 72-inch) bed. When the bed is unfolded, the top becomes a welcome headrest. The urethane-filled upholstered frame is available in a number of materials to blend with any decor.

HIDE-A-BED CHAIR. A handsome, well-upholstered armchair is a welcome addition to any living room or den. When it hides a comfortable single bed, it can be even more appreciated. **Thonet** offers casters as an optional choice on all of its hide-a-bed chair styles, making them easy to move from one room to another, or simply to shift when you need to attack the dust beneath them. Convertible sofas are available to match most Thonet chair models.

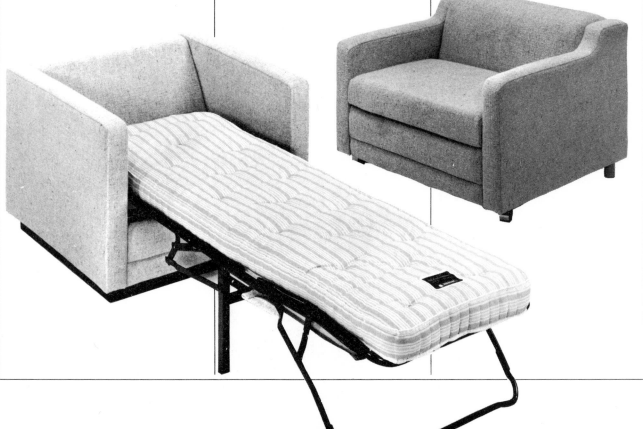

BED IN A BOX. Milo Baughman designed this ingenious upholstered table to match his modular seating units. Offered by **Thayer Coggin,** it is topped with stain-resistant laminate (available in a number of colors) and is offered in four sizes—from 47 to 71 inches in width. Beneath is a comparably sized mattress (from 37 to 61 inches wide) that is about 6 feet long. When the bed is pulled out, the table top becomes a useful headboard.

PART TIME ARMLESS CHAISE. Any chaise longue is an inviting place to recline at the end of a long day. Milo Baughman's upholstered chaise offers that comfort and more: it also hides a full double bed. Depending on the configuration of the room you plan to put it in, you can order the chaise with either a left- or right-opening bed; **Thayer Coggin** will then cover it in your choice of fabrics.

THAYER COGGIN

From its factories in rural North Carolina, Thayer Coggin produces a wide range of contemporary furniture for both home and office. Modular seating groups, chairs, and storage pieces are the company's forte, in designs ranging from traditional to postmodern. Many of Thayer Coggin's sofas and chairs—and even tables— can be ordered with hidden beds, adding to their flexibility and usefulness. Once you've selected the appropriate upholstered pieces, you can choose coverings from an almost infinite variety of materials.

CHAPTER 4

Sofas, Love Seats, and Benches

Daybeds and Love Seats

·

Sectional and Modular Sofas

·

Benches

Sofas, Love Seats, and Benches

With the exception of a confirmed hermit or two, we human beings are a gregarious lot. Even if we plan to live alone, chances are that one of the first items of furniture we purchase will be a sofa or daybed that can accommodate several people in comfort whenever the need arises. And because such furniture is usually quite sizeable and not inexpensive, we will select it with special care and with its overall proportions and their suitability to the space for which it's intended kept firmly in mind. Once that selection is made, other furnishings (occasional chairs, carpeting, tables, and lamps among them) can be chosen to complement it.

To those of us for whom space and mobility are paramount, a three- or four-cushion sofa will not be a practical choice, unless it hides a comfortable bed that gives it a second use. The multiple seating selections in this chapter, therefore, do not include large single units, though many of the manufacturers included can supply sofas in the same designs as the love seats or sectionals featured. Smaller-scaled and thus more portable modular sofas, love seats, and benches can provide ample seating without overpowering a too-small room or taking up more than their fair share of floor area. In addition, such pieces can be easily moved to a new spot without undue difficulty, whether you plan to relocate them across the room or across the country. Their smaller size makes them more flexible, as well, giving you more than one choice of placement and the luxury to rearrange the room if need or desire dictates.

Certainly the most flexible of multiple seating choices available today is the modular or sectional sofa. Many styles are available in several different modules, from straight-backed armless units to corner or one-armed pieces, enabling you to select a combination to fit your requirements. Some of the modules are curved, some angular. All give you the option of designing an individual arrangement that is exactly right for your room.

You can also choose from a wide variety of love seats, daybeds, and benches. Generally designed to seat at least two people with plenty of elbow room between them, each can be used singly or in groups as your requirements demand, providing cozy seating in living room or den. Most of the benches are compact enough to fit comfortably in the front hall or entrance way, but light enough to move to the living room or the dining room table when you need additional seating.

Daybeds and Love Seats

If a massive three- or four-cushion sofa doesn't suit your design plans or fit the available floor area in your living room, you might want to try a daybed or a pair of love seats instead. Either is generally constructed on a somewhat smaller and lighter scale than a sofa and thus offers a more flexible solution to arranging furniture in a constricted space. Most love seats will accommodate two people comfortably; a pair of them placed opposite each other, perhaps with a coffee table between them, provides an inviting place for good conversation over a drink or a buffet supper. Daybeds are so named because of their utility: most will convert from seating to bed with no wasted motion or effort simply by removing a few cushions. Contemporary designers have created many styles that combine utility with good-looking sophistication appropriate for virtually any decor.

ALLEGRO. Designer Michael Knoll emphasizes the semi-lunar form in a softly molded love seat with radius edges; the overall effect is one of luxurious relaxation. **Brayton International** offers Allegro in a number of upholstery fabrics; you might choose a contrasting color for the supporting frame.

GRAFFITI. Designed by Burkhard Vogtherr, the Graffiti (*right*) is a spare, yet luxurious, daybed available in a wide range of fabrics and leathers. **Brayton International** combines a slab cushion with low bolsters at each end, the whole supported by thin ash legs. The frame can be finished in gray, ebony, or a natural tone. In any fabric and finish, the daybed measures 81 inches in length by 28½ inches wide and stands just 18¾ inches tall.

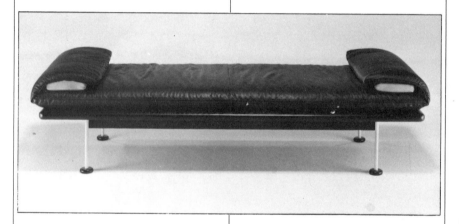

SHERWOOD GAMBE. The twin ratchet arms of **Placewares'** compact settee (*left*) adjust easily to any of six positions for reclining and sleeping as well as sitting. The steel frame is cushioned by a foam mattress covered in quilted cotton duck; two loose coordinating pillows are included. The Sherwood Gambe measures 59 inches in length with the arms raised; it opens to a 78-inch-long bed.

DOOR STORE

For the past thirty years, the Door Store has specialized in contemporary home furnishings which emphasize both good design and quality construction. Many of the company's pieces are selected with an eye to both practicality and portability. Among its daybeds and love seats, for instance, are a number which can be converted to beds any time you require extra sleeping room. Most Door Store furnishings are shipped knocked down, but can be assembled at home with a minimum of bother; heavier pieces often can be fitted with casters upon request.

LOVE SEAT AND SOFA. The understated design of the **Door Store**'s matching love seat and sofa is echoed in the upholstery: each cushion is covered in a gray, white, and black cotton weave that blends with the gray-finished wood frames. The sofa is 77 inches long; the love seat, 52 inches in length. Matching cocktail and end tables are also available; each of the pieces can be assembled quickly and, conversely, knocked down for storage if you need to make extra room.

AURA. Whether you choose to have it made up as a love seat, armchair, or three-cushion sofa, Paolo Piva's Aura is a plump, inviting design with compact lines well defined by self-welting or contrasting welting of a different fabric or color. **Stendig** offers the Aura in a choice of fabrics and leathers; the beech legs can be finished in any one of a variety of color tones to complement the upholstery selected.

MISINTO. One of **Greenbaum**'s newest imports from Busnelli of Italy (*below*), this innovative love seat is as practical as it is handsome. All cushion covers are removable for cleaning, and front rollers make it a breeze to move from one location to another. The wide, flat arms conceal turning trays that can be pulled out whenever you need them; detachable arm cushions can be moved to the back for use as comfortable head rests.

DAYBED. The romantic look of **Amisco**'s steel-framed daybed belies its practical side: the back can be removed, converting it into a generously proportioned single bed (82 inches by 42 inches). The frame can be finished in your choice of colors (you supply the mattress and decorative pillows); the matching trundle shown tucked beneath the daybed is optional (see page 61). As is the case with most of Amisco's home furnishings, the daybed is easy to disassemble for storage when you don't need it.

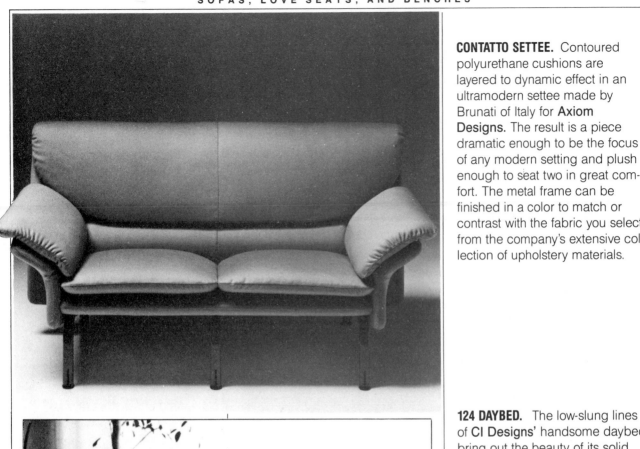

CONTATTO SETTEE. Contoured polyurethane cushions are layered to dynamic effect in an ultramodern settee made by Brunati of Italy for **Axiom Designs.** The result is a piece dramatic enough to be the focus of any modern setting and plush enough to seat two in great comfort. The metal frame can be finished in a color to match or contrast with the fabric you select from the company's extensive collection of upholstery materials.

124 DAYBED. The low-slung lines of **CI Designs'** handsome daybed bring out the beauty of its solid ash construction. Fully 79 inches long, it features removable bolsters so that it can be instantly converted from a comfortable multiple seating unit to a roomy bed whenever you need extra sleeping space.

Sectional and Modular Sofas

There is no doubt that sectional, or modular, sofas, offer the greatest flexibility in furniture arrangement. Once you have chosen a handsome seating group that fits your current needs, it can be easily adapted to conform to a new room should you move or wish to change its location within your home or apartment. Even if you don't move or have the luxury of several rooms to reconfigure, you can rearrange the pieces with the change of seasons or of mood. (You might want to place a cozy grouping in front of the hearth or wood stove during the winter months, but move it to a separate location in summer.) You could even elect to split up the units to form several groupings instead of one. No matter what arrangement of pieces you envision, you'll find any number of handsome designs and styles to choose among.

SISTEMA 61. Cubes of injected molded polyurethane can be arranged in virtually endless configurations according to the shape of your room and the effect you wish to create. Once you have positioned them to your satisfaction, they are secured with chrome-plated metal brackets. **Castelli Furniture** will upholster both seat modules and back/armrest modules in your choice of textiles. The seat modules measure 24 inches square by 16 inches high; the back/armrest modules, 27½ inches high, 24 inches wide, and 12 deep.

HABANA SEATING. Designed by Stanley Jay Friedman for **Brueton Industries,** these plump, inviting armless units are stuffed with down and polyester for the ultimate in comfort. Each piece measures 27 inches wide by 36 deep and 29 high. No matter how many modules you decide to use, they can be upholstered in your choice of attractive, durable upholstery materials from the Brueton collection.

OTTAWA. Designed by DePas, D'Urbino, Lomazzi for **International Contract Furnishings,** the Ottawa modular sofa pieces are composed of dacron-filled cushions that rest on rugged steel frames and springs. All upholstery fabrics are secured with Velcro closures for easy removal. Nylon gripper feet hold the pieces steady on floor or rug. Choose among right- and left-arm units, armless pieces, ottomans, and two- and three-seat sofas.

DAMIER. All of the modules in the Damier grouping—corners, armless units, and curved pie-shaped units which create the arrangement shown—are carefully scaled to fit small seating areas. (The biggest is just 31 inches in width.) Once you have selected a configuration to suit your room and have set the modules in place, leather straps with loops attached to the front and back of each connecting piece can be secured by means of a specially designed metallic pin. **Arconas** constructs its Damier collection with frames of steel tubing. A choice of fabrics and leathers is available; all materials zip on and off easily for cleaning.

THAYER COGGIN MODULAR SEATING. The basic angularity of **Thayer Coggin**'s modular units is offset by their gently rounded backs and softly molded cushions. Both armless and corner units are 34 inches wide and the armless units and matching ottoman (not shown), 31 inches in width. Choose among Thayer Coggin's wide range of upholstery fabrics. Specify model numbers 1850, 1851, and 1852 for ottoman, armless unit, and corner unit, respectively.

Benches

The lowly bench has come a long way from its humble beginnings; until well after the Middle Ages, it was one of the few pieces of furniture available to the commoners who were then (and are now) the vast majority of the populace. The craftsmanship that goes into many of the benches available today is such, however, that even the most discerning aristocrat could find a number of them appealing, to say nothing of the rest of us. In addition to their good looks, benches are among the more portable of home furnishings. Usually small enough to fit into an area too cramped to accommodate a padded love seat or sofa, they still provide seating for two or three people and can be moved from room to room to seat an overflow crowd. Some, such as the Ikea design shown below, even offer extra storage space beneath their seats.

PINE BENCH. It would be easy to think of a number of places where **Ikea**'s simple pine bench would be useful, since its hinged seat hides an ample storage area. Put it in an entry hall to hold boots and umbrellas; in a child's room to organize a toy collection; in a roomy eat-in kitchen to store napery or utensils: the list is limited only by your needs and your imagination.

CHERRY AND WALNUT BENCH. Tom **Wessells** was inspired by the ancient art of Japanese temple joinery to craft this cherry and walnut bench. Roughly five feet in length, the bench has no fasteners holding it together; the intricate shapes of the temple joints secure the contrasting wood pieces and contribute to the unusual design. The interlocking pieces come apart easily for storage.

TOM WESSELLS

Tom Wessells is a gifted artist whose medium is fine wood. Many of his original furniture designs have been exhibited at galleries and museums throughout the Mid-Atlantic area. Working in his Virginia studio, Wessells concentrates on special commissions and has executed a wide range of furnishings and architectural details, from side chairs and coffee tables to highboys, sofas, and mantles.

DEACON BENCH. The classic lines of **Strictly Country**'s deacon bench would make it suitable for either a period or a contemporary interior. It is available in either a four- or five-foot length (specify model S10019 and S10020, respectively) and can be made of either oak or cherry, as you prefer.

CALDWELL BENCH/SETTEE. **Steven Caldwell** has been honored with many awards for his furniture designs, all of which are made only to custom order. His careful artistry is evident in the graceful lines of this settee, whose ash seat is suspended on a bentwood laminated frame. Caldwell will upholster the seat in a fine hand-woven wool or will supply another fabric you specify.

PRINCETON BENCH. Artisan **Peter Korn** invites commission work and is happy to create one-of-a-kind furniture to your order. Among the handsome pieces he can supply from stock is the Princeton bench, whose angular sections are wedded using three different wood joints: mortise and tenon, inverted tenon, and sliding dovetail. Made of oak with a rich tung-oil finish, the bench measures 60 inches wide by 35 high and is 21 inches deep.

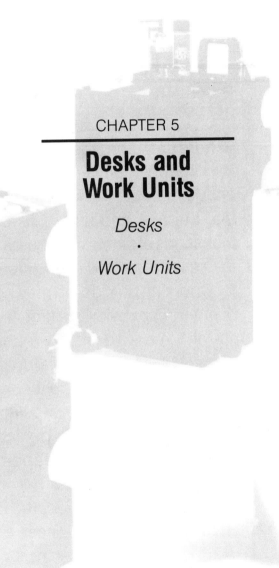

CHAPTER 5

Desks and Work Units

Desks

·

Work Units

Desks and Work Units

*T*here are hundreds of thousands of people throughout North America for whom a 9 to 5 office job is anathema. Yet practical considerations usually dictate that the rent and utility bills be paid. And there are thousands of others who must start to earn extra income to help support the ever-increasing cost of living, but for whom an outside job may not be possible because of other responsibilities. For all of those people, an office at home is a necessity of daily life. Chances are that the rest of us need a quiet space in which to balance the checkbook, prepare the tax return, and organize the pile of bills (paid or unpaid) which accumulates so rapidly. Yet many office supply companies feature desks and other work units more appropriate for a boardroom than for the corner of the living room or spare bedroom that has to be commandeered for the job. Many of their offerings are massive pieces of furniture that not only look inappropriate parked next to the guest bed or parlor sofa, but usurp too much space in the bargain.

Fortunately, as demand for small-scale yet practical office furniture increases, home furnishing suppliers are augmenting their repertoires with a variety of desks, typing tables, and work tables specifically geared to personal use. Many companies offer understated designs

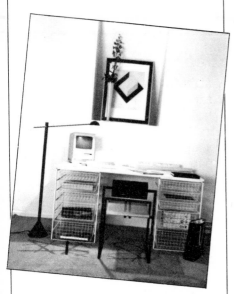

that will blend unobtrusively with the other accoutrements of personal life, yet are as functional as they are handsome. There are desks that can be ordered to match bedroom furniture and can double easily as both work area and dressing table. Many contemporary desks can be folded or disassembled for storage if you need extra room. Others feature convenient hinged flaps that can be raised to increase the work surface, but that, when folded, don't take up a lot of unnecessary space that you would rather have available for other functions. Still others are modular designs that permit you to choose exactly the right components for your purpose.

Even if you don't need a complete office that will allow you to perform a full- or part-time job within your home or apartment, you might relish the idea of having a spacious work table on hand for special projects or hobbies. If you are reluctant to apportion the amount of space required on a full-time basis, or if the confines of your living quarters make it impossible to do so, there is still a solution. In fact, there are a number of possibilities to choose among. For example, many drafting and art tables are designed to fold compactly so that they can be removed from the room when the project is completed. Yet when you set them up, they provide ample work space and can be angled to just about any position that the task dictates.

The key to all of the desks and work units featured on the following pages is their flexibility and their utility—two benefits which make them especially welcome additions to just about any home environment.

Desks

Whether you are clipping coupons, answering mail, paying the monthly bills, or writing a book, you might like a special place to keep all of the paper those and many other tasks tend to generate. Even if your space is limited, you don't have to spread the mess out on the dining table and put it away when it's time for lunch. There are a number of compact, utilitarian desks available that will enable you to organize your paperwork with ease and provide plenty of writing space in the bargain. Some have hinged flaps that provide lots of elbow room when raised; when lowered, however, they allow you to stash the desk in an unobtrusive corner out of the line of traffic. All the desks featured here have in common the generous drawer space they provide for the storage of check stubs, correspondence, and the rest of the paperwork that is one of the curses of daily living.

SLIDE-TOP DESK. When its hinged flap is down, the **Door Store**'s teak veneer desk is just 45½ inches wide. Whenever you need additional space to spread out papers, just slide the top over to bring up the flap, and you'll have a generous 65 inches of width. Two convenient drawers under the top include a letter-size file for keeping important correspondence and bills in order.

DANISH KNOCK-DOWN DESK.
Finished in white PVC for easy maintenance, and sporting bright red D handles for contrast, the **Door Store**'s contemporary desk is just 47 inches wide, yet it includes three shallow drawers at one side, a bookcase at the other, and plenty of space for your knees in-between. Imported from Denmark, the desk can be ordered with a separate, matching four-shelf bookcase. Both pieces knock down easily for storage.

BON MARCHÉ

Bon Marché imports many of its contemporary home furnishings from Europe, where some of today's most innovative designs are being created. Whether you are able to visit one of its retail outlets in the New York or Washington, D.C., area, or do your shopping by mail, you'll find a selection of modern furniture and housewares broad enough to furnish an entire home or apartment. Bon Marché specializes in knock-down pieces that are easy to put together but that can be stored flat until you need them.

FOLD-DOWN DESK. A white polyvinyl veneer finish makes **Bon Marché**'s fold-down desk easy to clean and relatively impervious to wear. Its hinged flap, supported on sturdy folding legs, makes it a good choice for tight spaces. And the base is fitted with casters so that you can move the piece easily whenever you need to open it fully for letter writing or bill paying. Two roomy drawers are included.

HANGING FILE DESK. A hinged lid (shown open) built into the top of **Bon Marché**'s teak veneer desk hides a deep hanging file drawer that runs the full width of the piece—a generous five feet. Since the drawer is secreted at the back of the desk, it won't cause you to bark your shins every time you sit down, and the hardware won't interfere with your writing space. When the drawer lid is closed, it provides an even bigger expanse of work area to spread out on.

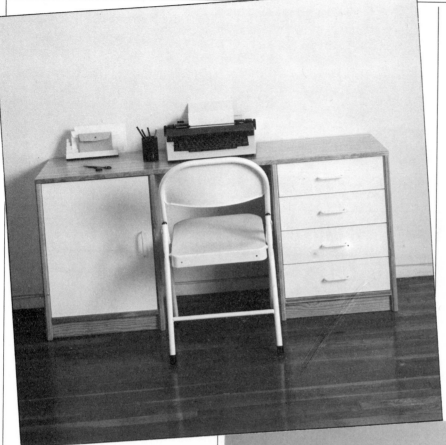

VARIANTE DESK/DRESSING TABLE.

Part of an entire system of bedroom furniture and storage pieces imported by **Conran's** from Portugal, the Variante desk/dressing table is composed of white melamine and natural pine veneer and fitted with simple white D handles. Use it as a work space or as a dressing table—or as both if you're cramped for space. Conran's packs it flat for shipment, but it can be assembled in minutes and no tools are required. The piece measures 47 inches in width by 19 inches deep.

TECHLINE SYSTEM. The desk and typing return shown at right are just two possibilities you can select from a wide range of modular Techline components that **Placewares** has available. Finished in white, gray, or oak-veneer melamine over a composite wood core, the components can be assembled easily; all you'll need is a screwdriver. The matching two-drawer file on casters would be an especially practical addition to the modular system, but would be equally useful on its own.

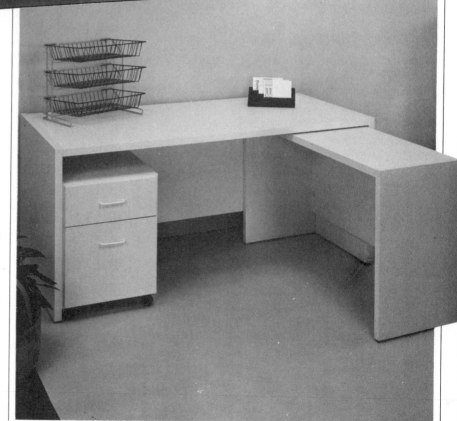

CHARRETTE

Founded as an architectural supply store in 1964, Charrette specializes in professional design materials and equipment. The furniture it offers is geared to use by draftsmen and other design professionals, and includes drafting tables, desks, chairs, lamps, and complete file systems. Yet many of the company's furnishings have great practical application for the home office, as they are modular units which can be adapted to serve a wide variety of functions.

REFERENCE TABLE. Part of **Charrette**'s Modular Furniture System, this spacious table is made of ivory-colored melamine panels trimmed with natural oak. The two-drawer cabinet is optional and can be attached to either side of the table, a special boon if you are left-handed. The top

drawer is a roomy 6½ inches deep; the bottom accommodates standard letter files. Matching drafting tables, computer tables, and free-standing shelves are also available. All are shipped knocked down and can be quickly assembled with ordinary household tools.

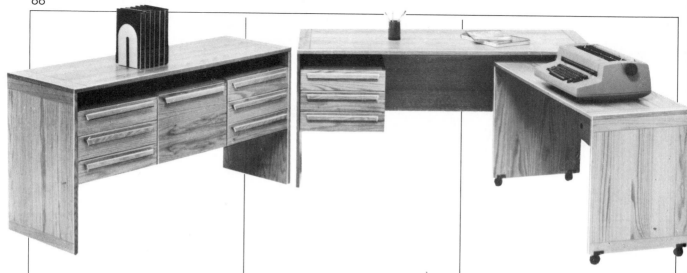

DESK/CREDENZA. Because of its modular construction, the credenza shown above at left can be transformed into the desk next to it simply by removing its center and one of its side drawer units. However, if you find that the more storage you have, the more clutter you collect, and therefore prefer a more Spartan way of working, you might opt to have the desk without any file modules added. The matching typing table can be rolled partly under the desk to conserve space. **Workbench** offers these knock-down modular units in either teak or oak veneer.

ELFA DESK. If you can't find a ready-made desk to suit your needs, why not build one that's exactly the right size and has just the right number of storage bins? The Elfa system offered by **Lynk** and **Placewares** is designed so that you can select as many pull-out baskets as you require, pick an appropriate top (in birch veneer or Formica laminate), and put all of the components together using only a hammer. Casters can be fitted to the connector legs for greater mobility.

Work Units

A sturdy work or drafting table that provides ample room for drawing, writing, and other endeavors is a handy adjunct to most home furnishings. It may be a necessity, in fact, if you work out of your home. If you are blessed with a roomy garage, basement, or spare room, you can set up such a table with impunity and not worry about the floor space it usurps. If not, you might want to consider one that can be folded or knocked down to slip in a closet after you've finished the current project. Whether you choose a natural wood table or one with a maintenance-free polyvinyl finish, there are a number of utilitarian, attractive models available that will further your pursuit of either avocation or career.

COMPUTER TABLE. Although the **Door Store** designed its solid oak table especially to accommodate a personal computer, you might find it equally practical to use as a desk because of its generous work space (30 by 40 inches) and handy extra shelf. The height of the entire piece is 37 inches and the overall width 44 inches. Like most of the Door Store's home furnishings, it is shipped knocked down and assembles—or disassembles—easily, using only a wrench.

CAMBRIDGE. Steel struts lock into place to support the legs of the Cambridge drawing table, but collapse easily when you want to fold it up for storage. The white laminated top adjusts from 33 to 44 inches in height and can be set at any angle from 0 to 90 degrees. **Charrette** finishes the steel frame in black or white baked enamel and includes two self-leveling feet that will make short work of the most uneven floor surface.

LOFFE/BENKE. Ikea's Loffe trestles, made of solid pine, adjust to 11 different heights (from 25½ to 37 inches). They can be teamed, as shown, with the Benke pine top, which is available in two rectangular sizes or in a circular model roughly 36 inches in diameter. Or choose a different top or base from Ikea's wide selection and put together a sturdy work table that suits your individual needs.

BMC FOLD-AWAY TABLE. When set up, the BMC table features a sizable work space (42 by 30 inches) that can be adjusted from an angled to a flat position at your pleasure. Yet the heavy round tubing base folds compactly, so that you can store the unit easily when it is no longer required. Although this **Placewares** offering is certainly suitable for professional draftsmen, you might find other uses for it. Because of its portability, it could easily function as an extra desk or brunch table if the need arises.

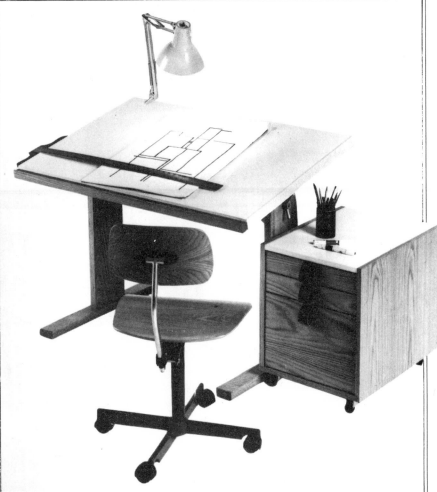

DRAFTING TABLE AND ROLLING FILE. Both the height and tilt of this solid-oak drawing table from **Workbench** can be adjusted to any number of positions. The top is surfaced with a white plastic laminate, as is the top of the matching oak file cabinet which can be rolled out when needed and tucked under the table when the work is done. The cabinet features three roomy drawers that provide ample storage for pens, pencils, and paper.

WORKBENCH

Workbench stores offer a wide range of contemporary home furnishings that are both well designed and well made. To that end, the company makes careful selections from the stock of a number of innovative European manufacturers. But not all of its furnishings are imported. Because the North American lifestyle sometimes has unique requirements, Workbench commissions exclusive designs from domestic manufacturers who will produce those designs to its specifications.

FOLDING DRAFTING TABLE. The Door Store's drafting table features an adjustable white Formica top and steel legs finished in black epoxy. The table folds flat for compact storage, as does the Door Store's equally useful metal chair.

BOBY UTILITY STAND. Designed by Joe Columbo for **Charrette,** this modular utility stand features deep storage wells that will easily accommodate mailing tubes, rolled posters, or rolls of gift wrap, and is fitted with open shelves and shallow pivoting drawers. Depending on the model you select, you can have as many as 2 tube wells, 3 storage shelves, and 9 drawers, yet the largest stand is only 29 inches high and roughly 16 inches square. Most models are available in a wide range of colors, including brown, yellow, and green; all come in white, black, or red.

CHAPTER 6

Shelving and Cabinets

*Freestanding
Components*

·

Hanging Components

Shelving and Cabinets

Do you collect books? Records? Tapes for your new VCR? Porcelain figurines? Even if you aren't acquisitive by nature and are relatively scrupulous about shedding unwanted or outmoded items, you have probably found that the objects of daily life tend to accumulate at an alarming rate, increasing in inverse proportion to your available space and your wallet. Once-commodious shelves overflow and the resulting clutter spreads to areas that you had intended to maintain in Spartan order. Especially if you're an incorrigible pack rat, you may think that the situation is hopeless. But it needn't be. Nor do you have to spend a major part of your household budget on custom-made shelving and cabinets.

Contemporary furniture designers are creating imaginative and effective systems to display and store the objects we are passionate about, while remaining alert to budgetary considerations and aesthetics. One result of their efforts is a wide range of interchangeable cabinet and shelving components flexible enough to accommodate anything from a spare coat closet to a complete sound and video system. Another is the availability of portable open shelves that can be set up or knocked down according to need. Whether you prefer the con-

temporary look of white enamel or a more traditional oak or walnut veneer, you can select a complete wall system—or just one unit—that is right for any room.

Among the most versatile designs available are modular systems which can be stacked *ad infinitum*. Most begin with a basic cube, to which can be added shelves, drawers, and doors in endless combinations. One of the major benefits of such systems is that the individual components are generally quite compact, enabling you to arrange them in a configuration that is a perfect fit for the space you have available. Another is their flexibility: should you move, or should you want to rearrange your floor plan, the cubes can be shifted at will. A wall system could thus become a room divider, or could be split to fill two walls smaller than the one for which it was originally intended. And when you need still more storage room, you'll probably be able to add matching components inexpensively.

If the layout of your rooms makes a free-standing wall system an awkward choice (you might not have an un-broken expanse of wall available), or if you prefer a more permanent option, there are a number of wall-hung systems to choose from. Most widely available are open shelves that depend from vertical supports attached to the wall. A series of horizontal brackets is clipped to the supports at random intervals to accommodate the shelves. Such an option is extremely flexible: you could, for instance, install a single shelf over a doorway, run a group from floor to ceiling, or select any other com-bination that makes sense for the wall space you have to work with. The width, depth, and height of the shelves can be varied according to the size of the books and other items you plan to display. Some designs allow you to add closed cabinets and other modular units in an arrangement tailored to your personal needs.

Freestanding Components

One of the most attractive features of a well-designed house or apartment is a set of built-in bookcases or cabinets that will house the ever-increasing number of possessions most of us seem to collect. Unfortunately, such built-ins are not ubiquitous in modern life. And even if you are fortunate enough to live in a home which contains ample cabinets as part of its interior architectural detailing, there is one major drawback: you can't take them with you if you move. Luckily, there are a number of ingenious freestanding wall systems and shelves available that are both well designed and portable. Some models have the look of built-in units and thus can add immeasurably to your decor while augmenting your storage space. Others are modular pieces that will serve equally well along a wall or can be used as room dividers to give you a good deal of flexibility in furniture arrangement.

ENTERTAINMENT CENTER. Hand-crafted of kiln-dried Southern yellow pine, the **Pine Factory**'s modular stackable units each measure 32 inches wide by 20 deep and 31 high, providing plenty of room for stereo components or a television. The basic unit features two adjustable shelves to which a pair of hinged doors can be added; instead of the shelves you might select three roomy drawers.

PALASET STORAGE. Placewares and **Conran's** both provide the versatile, inexpensive Palaset system. Its basic component is a black or white cube that measures 13½ inches on all sides. By adding a door, four drawers, or extra shelves, you can create a virtually unlimited arrangement that can be adjusted to fit any wall. Once you have decided on the right configuration to suit your needs, attach the cubes using the connectors supplied. For greater stability, you might elect to screw the units to the wall.

TEAK BOOKCASE. A trio of handsome teak bookcases, each measuring 34 inches wide by 71 inches high, makes an attractive wall system that will display treasured volumes in style but not usurp much floor space (each is less than 12 inches deep). Or use the units separately, if you prefer. Each has one stationary shelf and three adjustable ones. If there are items you'd rather keep hidden, **Scandinavian Design** can add a set of doors to each bookcase.

HAGERWOOD MODULES. Each of the rounded open modules in the Hagerwood system is 16 inches deep; the length and width can vary from 8 by 16 inches to 24 by 32 inches. Because the modules are shipped knocked down, you can select exactly the right sizes for the items you want to display. Simply snap the pieces together (first applying a bit of household glue for extra stability), then glue each unit in place. **Hagerwood** provides its modular wall system in a natural wood finish so that you can apply any color or stain you like. One module alone could be used as a table; a group could become a room divider.

MAGIC. This teak veneer entertainment unit from **Van Pelt** is specifically designed to organize both audio equipment and a television/VCR combination, and to provide ample shelf space for records, video cassettes, and tapes. Duo-fold doors hide the TV; audio components fit in a sliding shelf which allows ready access when you want to put on a record; and the entire cabinet is shipped flat to be assembled easily at home.

RIVIERA. Van Pelt gives the name "Riviera" to an entire line of ready-to-assemble wall units that can be put together in just about any configuration you require. At left are a bookcase unit, drop-down desk with cabinet, and wardrobe that provides extra closet space. Available in rosewood or oak veneer with solid wood moldings and trim, the units can be connected with special hardware that gives extra stability to each piece. Display units with tempered safety glass fronts are available, as are cabinets with solid doors.

WHITE RIVIERA. Van Pelt's white laminated Riviera cabinets (*above, left*) might be a better choice for an informal lifestyle than its wood-veneer models. Varied cabinet widths are available, and components can be chosen from a wide range of options, including a drop-lid library, adjustable open shelves, cabinets, and glass-fronted doors. Grooved moldings add a distinctive touch to the clean, contemporary lines. As is the case with all Van Pelt Lifestyle models, the units are shipped knocked down for quick assembly without nails or glue.

STAR COMBI STORAGE. Designed in Sweden and made in Germany for **Workbench,** the modular storage system shown below is finished in white lacquer. Among the components you may select are tall, narrow bookshelves, bedroom chests, desks, drop fronts, glass or solid doors, extra shelves, and sets of drawers. While the Star Combi system is not meant to house heavy audiovisual equipment, it will accept virtually anything else you have to store.

NACKA. **Ikea**'s lacquered particle-board cubes can be stacked on the floor or hung from the wall. The basic cube is 31 inches wide, 13¾ inches deep, and 15¾ inches high. To it can be added four drawers with hardwood guide rails, a set of record dividers, or shelves. The result is an extremely flexible and inexpensive wall storage system that can fill a variety of requirements. The cubes are available in white or bright red.

AN OPEN AND SHUT CASE. This beechwood bookcase is an innovative one-piece design from the **Door Store:** it sets up in seconds and folds flat for easy storage. Perfect for small budgets, weekend homes, or for a college student to take along as a practical adjunct to a dormitory room, the Open and Shut bookcase has an extra advantage—you can stack several for added height without usurping too much valuable floor space.

IKEA

Ikea was founded in Sweden in 1943 and has since opened many stores throughout Europe and, more recently, North America. Everything the company sells from its home furnishings outlets in Pennsylvania, Virginia, and Canada is geared to the Swedish ideal of a home that is furnished with informal, comfortable pieces as attractive as they are practical. All of Ikea's designs originate within the company; they have in common the principle that the finished piece can be packed flat and shipped disassembled for the customer to put together at home. The result is furniture that is comparatively inexpensive, yet high in quality and durability.

IVAR. A solid pine shelving system, Ivar comes in a choice of two depths and three heights, with lots of extra fittings to make its uses almost limitless. You can add drawers, two-door cabinets, clothes rails, record shelves, and desk or adjustable work tops as you see fit. The result is a warm, casual shelving system that will accommodate just about anything you have to store in it. Depending on your needs, the Ivar system could be arrayed along a wall or used as a high or low room divider. **Ikea** leaves the pine unfinished for you to stain or paint as you like, but it would be equally attractive with just a clear varnish applied for protection.

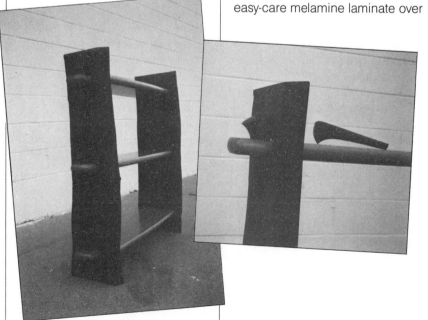

TECHLINE. Select the components you require from Techline's wide array of doors, drawers, cabinets, shelves, and desk tops. All basic units are 18 or 36 inches wide and 18 inches deep; they come in six heights, ranging from 17 to 86 inches. The modules are made of easy-care melamine laminate over a composite wood core (the laminate comes in white or gray; many pieces are also available in an oak laminate veneer). Once you've made your choice, **Placewares** will ship each unit flat for you to assemble at home or will assemble them for you at a slight additional charge.

WESSELLS BOOKSHELF. Hand-crafted from an unusual combination of fine woods, **Tom Wessells'** inventive bookshelf is as practical as it is handsome. The ends are of walnut; the shelves, of white oak (with a urethane finish); and the wedges which hold it together, of rosewood. The bookshelf, which measures 40 inches wide by 36 high and is 10 inches deep, can be easily disassembled for storage.

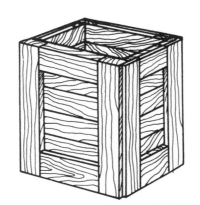

PLACEWARES

Maynard Hale Lyndon and Lu Wendel Lyndon, who founded Placewares in 1978, are dedicated to providing help for people who need to make the most of their living and working spaces. In half a dozen stores spread throughout the Boston area and in their comprehensive catalogue, the Lyndons feature accessories, hardware, furnishings, and fixtures that offer practical solutions to space problems. If you need additional help, Placewares offers a planning service that puts special emphasis on the modular shelving and cabinet systems that are one of its specialties.

KARTEL STACKING DRAWERS. White modular plastic stacking drawers are joined by connector pins and can be positioned to open from any side. Each drawer unit is 16½ inches square and 5½ inches high. **Placewares** offers the drawers, lids, and optional casters separately for great versatility. You might pile a few next to a bed, or arrange several stacks along a wall as shown (*above, right*). Because you can select exactly the right number of drawers to suit your requirements, you might find them especially useful to fit a tall, narrow space. Conversely, a cramped, low area under a dormer or in an attic that won't accommodate a more conventional bureau or cabinet would take a number of the Kartel drawers with ease.

PLANTER BOX. This sturdy, solid-pine box could certainly be used as a planter, or as a handsome receptacle for lots of other things. But a group turned on their sides can easily be arranged in vertical and horizontal configurations to suit your storage needs and your available space. Offered by the **Pine Factory,** the box measures 15 inches on a side and is 16 inches high.

GRAFFITI. English designer Rodney Kinsman has won deserved acclaim as the creator of functional, handsome metal furniture. His Graffiti shelving components, distributed by **Bieffe U.S.A.**, are of steel construction finished with epoxy paint in a choice of white, gray, black, yellow, red, aqua, or green. The various components are easy to put together; no installation is necessary, as the finished unit leans sturdily against the wall.

LEANING BOOK SHELF. No avid reader ever has enough shelf space; books seem to multiply as rapidly as coat-hangers for those of us to whom they are an essential not far removed from breathing. **Curtis Erpelding**'s solution to the space problem is this ingenious knockdown book shelf, shown both disassmbled (*top right*) and in its finished state. Erpelding crafts the piece in Douglas fir and makes it available in 4-foot or 6-foot lengths. Either size is easy to put together and takes minimum storage room when dismantled.

STAX SHELVING. The simplicity of the bookcase illustrated below is deceptive: it's actually just one unit of an expandable system offered by **The Pottery Barn** that can be arranged in any number of configurations—both in height and in width—to fit your particular needs. The laminated particleboard shelves fit together easily by means of an ingenious peg system, so assembly takes only minutes.

STACKING BOOKCASE. Curtis **Erpelding**'s furniture is intended, as he says, for "that individual who wants elegant yet practical solutions for modern living with its mobility and smaller spaces." That is certainly a description that fits most of us. His Douglas fir bookcases, shown both assembled and knocked down, can be stacked to whatever height is needed. The design, which Curtis admits was inspired by the old-fashioned barrister bookcases popular a century ago, is a classic that would look well with virtually any decorating scheme.

KUBUS STORAGE. Available in pine veneer or dramatic black lacquer finish, the Kubus system from **Conran's** is imported from Sweden. The basic cube unit measures 27 inches in both height and width and 14½ inches deep. You can add shelves, wood (or glass) doors, or drawers to each module, then stack any number to create an appropriate wall unit to suit your space and storage requirements.

NADIA BOOKCASE. Made of unfinished beech that you can paint, stain, or leave natural, this useful open bookcase can be stacked for extra height, or you might want to use several side by side. A gently curved three-shelf corner unit is also offered by **Conran's.** Each model folds flat for storage when not required, an especially practical feature that makes the Nadia more portable than most comparable bookshelves.

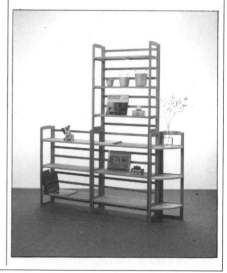

CONRAN'S

Twenty years ago, Terence Conran opened his first home furnishings store in Britain; now there are more than a dozen Conran's outlets in the north-eastern United States alone, and the company runs a thriving mail order business to serve customers in other parts of North America. Its enormous success is due in large part to Terence Conran's emphasis on sophisticated contemporary furniture that is well designed, reasonably priced, and flexible. Among the company's major offerings are knock-down shelving and cabinet systems that can be set up in various configurations depending on available space and room arrangement.

ARCTIC WALL UNIT. Finished in white lacquer or natural ash veneer, the Arctic wall unit from **Conran's** (*above, left*) is composed of three storage bays. Each 71-inch-tall bay features two fixed and two adjustable shelves, plus a special storage extra. The first has four spacious drawers; the second, a drop-leaf mid-section to use as a bar or small desk; and the third, a two-shelf enclosed cupboard. The three units may be clipped together as shown or used separately in different parts of a room or even in different rooms.

EUROFORM DIVISION BOOKCASES. These metal-frame bookcases afford a great deal of flexibility because of their light structure. They feature rounded melamine shelves and wicket-shaped frames. The frames are available in a choice of eight colors; the shelves, in white or black. **Origlia** offers four different models which stand from $43\frac{1}{3}$ to $78\frac{2}{3}$ inches tall, depending on the number of shelves you select.

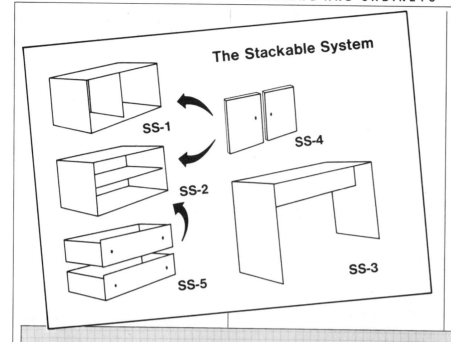

The Stackable System

SS-1

SS-4

SS-2

SS-5

SS-3

STACKABLES. Five basic components (*left*) comprise the Stackables system of furniture modules—two stacking units, a desk, drawers, and doors can be combined in various ways to create an arrangement such as the one shown below or can be configured to your taste and your available wall space. Since the units stack individually, they can be moved around whenever the mood strikes. **StackAShelf** offers the system in an oak or beige veneer or in a combination of the two. All modules are packed flat for quick assembly; the only tool you'll need will be a screwdriver.

Hanging Components

While freestanding shelves may be the optimum choice if you aren't comfortable with hammer or screwdriver, wall-hung components offer a great deal of flexibility and can often save space in the bargain. (Even if your job makes it likely that you will move fairly often, you needn't be overly concerned with the screw or nail holes you've made—it's amazing what a little spackle can do.) Hanging systems come in a wide range of widths, depths, and heights so that they can be tailored to fit any available wall space, regardless of the radiators or window openings that must be skirted. Infrequently used items can be placed on shelves above head height, freeing more floor area for other furnishings.

MORE RAKKS. The wall-mounted cabinets and open shelves shown above give some indication of the variety inherent in **Rangine**'s Rakks Space Management System. The cabinets mount in 32-inch modules on wall standards and are available in a number of configurations: both 4-inch and 8-inch drawers may be combined in one module; 2-door cabinets in another; and open shelves in still another.

RAKKS. Probably the simplest components of the ingenious Rakks wall system are the bookshelves shown above. Wall-mounted standards with adjustable brackets permit you to support as many shelves as you need and to adjust them to a height that will accommodate the tallest or shortest objects in your collection. **Rangine Corporation** makes the supports available in either aluminum or black finish; the shelves, along with other Rakks modules, in black or white laminate or red oak veneer.

RANGINE CORPORATION

Rangine Corporation is a specialist in the engineering and production of inventive storage modules with innumerable applications for both office and home. No matter their intended purpose, all of the firm's components, offered under the name "Rakks Space Management System," are designed to be attached to wall-mounted brackets or floor-to-ceiling poles that provide support for even the heaviest objects. You may choose a system of drawers or shelves, a drafting board (with a lamp to illuminate it), a specially designed computer work station, or any combination that is just right for your needs. Several possibilities are shown on this and the following page.

AND STILL MORE RAKKS. Whether you need a solid wall of cabinets to store clothing and linens or a more open design that permits the display of your sculpture collection, **Rangine**'s Rakks system can fill the bill. Narrow drawers will easily hold jewelry and other minutia; larger ones, bulkier items. A compact bar cabinet includes a drop-leaf door and a shelf for bottles; a dozen or so pieces of your finest stemware can be hung from a rack mounted on the inside top. If you're running an office at home, you can even have a special unit for your computer printer and a system of wall-mounted files—just about anything, in short, except the kitchen sink.

MAGAZINE RACK. If you relegate your magazine to a pile on the bookshelf, chances are you will find it difficult to locate them when you want them. On the other hand, if you keep them on a wall-mounted rack such as the one **Plexi-Craft** offers, not only will you rescue them from oblivion, but probably from dilapidation as well. The angled shelves keep the magazines neatly stacked and un-creased; the clear Plexiglas allows you to choose just the right one without undue neck-craning or rifling.

CHAPTER 7

Storage

*Closet Systems and
Wardrobes*

·

*Freestanding Storage
Units*

·

*Hanging Racks and
Utility Shelving*

Storage

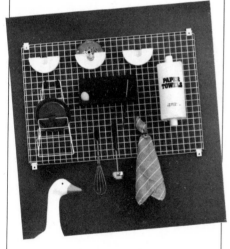

While a glass-front china closet, open wall system, or bookshelf makes an effective display of the treasures you want the world to see, there are many more practical, but perhaps less decorative, items you need from day to day that must be stored in some other fashion. Ideally, you'll already have found niches for all of them, including the kitchen utensils, household tools, garden supplies, current and off-season clothing, linens, and accessories. But since it isn't an ideal world, it's probable that there are storage areas in your home or apartment that could use some reorganization. And if you are among the majority, you don't have sufficient storage space to begin with.

The primary concern may be your clothes closets—or lack of them. If you have no budget limitations, you can hire one of the many excellent companies that specialize in custom systems tailored to fit your closets and all of the gear that must be stored in them. Or you can have a storage wall made especially for an appropriate room. While these options are good ones for homeowners, they generally result in permanent installations that have to be left behind if you move (they could add to the value of your home when you sell it, and most can't be adapted easily to fit in a new location). Luckily, there are many companies that offer both freestanding and easily installed closet systems flexible enough to move if you do

and to double your available closet space in the meantime.

Once you have fully utilized your clothes closets, you might want to cast a critical eye on other areas of your home. If you don't have sufficient cabinet space in your kitchen or bathroom (and who does?), you can augment it with some of the clever wall, door, or extra shelf components on the market. If extra shelving isn't the only answer to making your kitchen functional, you might want to consider one or more of the compact appliances specifically designed to save space (see Chapter 10).

If your gardening equipment, leisure gear, and household tools tend to wind up in a jumble on the floor of the garage, basement, or utility room, you can bring order to the chaos — and not by driving a bunch of nails into a convenient stud or two. There are flexible metal rack systems designed to hold all the gadgets you find essential to keeping your house or yard in order. Any one of them can be installed with only a few screws or masonry fasteners. Once you have the racks in place, you can rearrange the equipment as often as you like, using clip-on hooks specifically designed to hold the barbeque set, hedge clippers, lawn chairs, screwdrivers, and all the other paraphernalia vital to your do-it-yourself urges and/or to the enjoyment of your leisure time. Some of the rack systems even include wire shelves that can hold extra plant pots, fertilizer, peat moss, and bug spray.

There is a modular storage unit designed to accommodate everything from a bicycle to a case of soda, a soccer ball, or a box of laundry detergent. In short, no matter what oddly-shaped or awkward item you want to put neatly in its place, there is probably a ready-made storage component to do the job, since contemporary manufacturers seem able to anticipate our needs almost before we do.

Closet Systems and Wardrobes

The standard clothes closet, with its lone shelf above a single garment rod, is a poorly designed space that invites disorganization. All of the clothing, regardless of length, can be hung only from the one rod, leaving much of the space beneath to go to waste. Shoes wind up in a jumble on the floor with suitcases and carryalls that may not be needed for months. Hats, sweaters, spare blankets, and other paraphernalia are thrown on the shelf to be forgotten or misplaced. But there are possible solutions for the chaos. Any one of the systems featured on these pages can double the capacity of even the smallest closet. If you use one or more of them to reorganize each of your clothes closets but find that you need still more room, or you have no closets to work with, you might consider a freestanding wardrobe. There are a number of compact designs available, some of which include bureau storage in addition to space for hanging garments.

STACKING SHELVES. Two basic designs are available in **StackAShelf**'s freestanding closet shelf system. The horizontal two-shelf unit is 31 inches wide by 11½ high; the vertical, 30 inches high and a foot wide. Both are 11½ inches deep and can be stacked as high as you like to accommodate any items that need not be hung from a clothes bar. Finished in white vinyl for easy maintenance, both units are shipped flat; all hardware needed for quick assembly is included.

STORE MORE. Heavy particle board finished with a beige or simulated oak laminate composes the five basic units of the **Alumax** Store More system. Both horizontal and vertical shelves are offered, as are clothes poles (not shown—see page 141) which can be attached to the vertical unit on one side and to a wall or another vertical unit on the other. Both the vertical (30 or 36 inches high) and the horizontal (31 inches wide) units can be stacked for greater versatility.

VENTILATED SHELVING. The epoxy-coated steel construction of **Schulte**'s storage system permits air to circulate among the garments; open mesh baskets permit you to see what is stored within them. The basket drawers slide out on tracks for easy access; they are available in three widths and three depths to accommodate just about any article that needs to be put away. Once you've selected the baskets, choose one of Schulte's four frame sizes to support them; frames and baskets are freestanding, so you can change their location within the closet when you're in the mood to reorganize.

CLOSET MAXIMIZER. Part of **Dorfile**'s Ventaire System, this vinyl-coated steel shelving is available in three sizes to fit closets up to ten feet in width. The system is designed to provide ample space for shirts, jackets, and other short articles at one end, dresses and long coats at the other, and is bisected by half a dozen shelves. A slanted bottom rack keeps shoes off the floor. All hardware is included, as are the installation instructions (a drill and a screwdriver are the only tools required).

CLAIRSON INTERNATIONAL

Clairson International has manufactured Closet Maid storage systems for more than fifteen years, constantly adding to the available components and improving the system as a whole. In addition to various specialty shelving and wall, door, and cabinet racks, Clairson makes ventilated drawers that can be incorporated into any closet layout, eliminating the need for bureaus in a small bedroom or one-room apartment. Whether you need to organize a utility room, a pantry, or a walk-in closet such as the one shown below, Clairson makes components that are specifically tailored for the purpose. Clear instructions accompany all hardware, making the systems easy to install.

CLOSET MAID. Available in widths to fit any conventional closet, Closet Maid components include pre-cut shelving, pole supports, slanted shoe racks (*right*), and hardware. **Clairson International** includes complete instructions and a template that eliminates the need for time-consuming measuring and marking: just tack the template to the wall and drill the holes where indicated, then install the brackets and snap the shelves into place. All components are heavy-gauge steel with a smooth white epoxy coating.

STAY-NEAT HANGER SYSTEM. The basic components of the Stay-Neat system (*below*) are solid-oak brackets attached to vertical oak standards; as many as fifteen rubber-coated steel hangers can be inserted in each bracket. **Stay-Neat Closet Interiors** offers a variety of special garment hangers, or will supply swinging arms from which to hang your own. The company also makes a number of different storage cabinets with clear plastic drawers to organize shoes, sweaters, and other items. Optional accessories include tie and belt racks and shelf dividers.

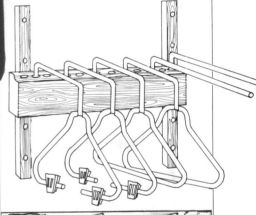

THE SWINGER SYSTEM. Each of the swinging steel arms attached to **Closet Systems'** wood and metal framework (*above*) can accommodate two standard hangers. The arms can be installed in every hole in the wooden bar to hold thin garments such as shirts and blouses; for bulkier items, you might want to skip every other hole. The bars come in two-foot lengths; each will hold a maximum of twenty-four arms. You can mount one on top of the other for shorter garments, or place several side by side for longer ones.

SINGLE WARDROBE. One of several handsome white oak models offered by **Thonet,** this single wardrobe is a mere 25½ inches wide. It can be ordered with 2 drawers beneath the clothes bar; if you need extra room, you might opt for a double (36-inch) cabinet, with or without a concealed 3-drawer chest.

VANITY WARDROBE. Thonet's compact wardrobe not only provides generous space for hanging clothes, but includes a three-drawer bureau (with an optional mirror above it) for lingerie and other items. The entire unit measures roughly 4 feet wide by 2 feet deep and is 6 feet high; the wardrobe compartment (with clothes rod installed) is 22 inches wide. Available in a variety of laminate finishes, the piece is fitted with adjustable leveling guides for extra stability on uneven floors. The wardrobe section can be fitted on either the left or right side of the cabinet, depending on where you plan to put it.

ATHENA. The Athena wardrobe from **Conran's** features a minimal contemporary design in white melamine veneer. Handles are available in white, or you might opt for aqua, yellow, or red for contrast. The double wardrobe is shipped knocked down for easy assembly; it measures $70\frac{7}{8}$ inches high by $38\frac{3}{4}$ wide and is $23\frac{5}{8}$ inches deep when set up. Matching bedroom pieces in the Athena group include a roomy 4- or 6-drawer chest, a bedside cabinet on casters, a desk, a dressing table, and a low 2-door cupboard.

Freestanding Storage Units

Even if you have only a one-room apartment in which to arrange all of the items necessary to your daily life, chances are there are areas that are not being properly utilized. Cabinets and closets crammed to bursting with piles of clothing and accessories can be reorganized to give you more room than you thought possible, and you don't have to get out the tools to install a custom-fitted system—a blessing to those of us who don't know one end of a screwdriver from the other. Whether you would like to revamp a cupboard below the sink or a spacious walk-in closet, you can augment your available space by adding one or more of the freestanding units featured on these pages. There are models specifically designed to fit in those constricted spaces that are usually left to collect dust; all are constructed of practical materials that are easy to clean and relatively impervious to normal wear.

CLOSET MAID DRAWER SYSTEMS. Clairson International's epoxy-coated steel-wire drawers come in several sizes and an assortment of frames so that you can choose a selection to fit any available space, whether it's in a closet or out in plain view. The drawers glide easily on wide, flat rims; you might crown them with a special laminated top for extra counter space.

ADD-A-SHELF. Rugged, durable heavy-gauge steel finished in beige, white, or brown composes these versatile shelves from **Quaker Industries.** The horizontal unit measures 15 inches in height by 30 wide and is 12 inches deep; the vertical, 30 inches high by 18 wide and 12 deep. All shelves can be inverted to provide a security lip that will prevent items from falling to the floor. Horizontal units can be stacked for greater flexibility; both models include vinyl feet to prevent scratching the floor, counter, or appliance top.

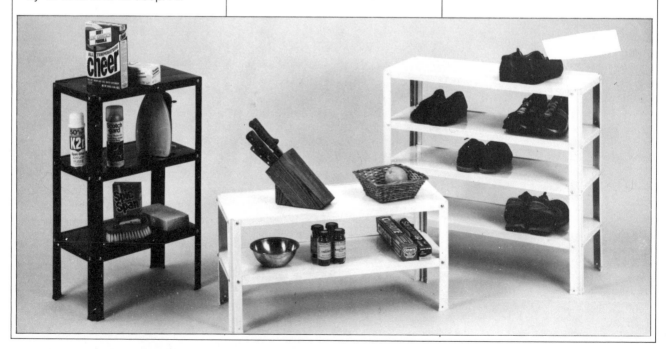

STOR-ALL. Unlike most cumbersome tall metal utility systems, **Quaker Industries'** Stor-All is scaled to fit easily in cramped spaces. Turn the unit one way for a width of only 12 inches, or change the position of the braces and you'll have a unit 18 inches wide. Composed of heavy-gauge steel with a laminated beige, white, or brown finish, the shelves would provide welcome extra storage in a tight spot in the laundry area, hallway, or garage, or could be slipped into a utility closet to organize cleaning materials and supplies.

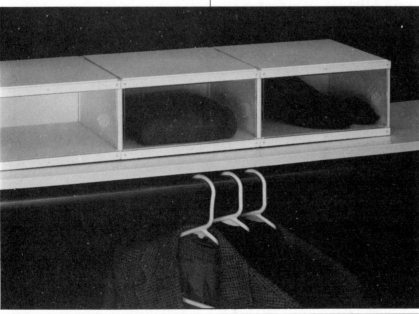

ROBOLO. Available in white, red, or black, the Robolo modular plastic units from **Placewares** snap together easily to make open shelves that can be stacked *ad infinitum*. With optional clear plastic doors attached, they become dust-free storage bins for off-season items. Each unit measures 9 by 12¾ inches and is 6 inches high—a compact size that makes them ideal for augmenting storage in cramped spaces such as kitchen cabinets or narrow utility closets. (You can assemble them with either the wide or narrow expanse facing front, depending on where you plan to use them.)

ROVEL TROLLEYS. If you need extra room for cleaning supplies or toiletries, or could use additional space for other household equipment that should be kept in an accessible location, you might consider one of the sturdy trolleys from **Better Houseware Corp.** (*above*). Available with either three or four shelves, the trolley is made of steel wire with a wipe-clean vinyl coating that can be ordered in red, white, blue, yellow, or brown.

BASICS TROLLEY. Made in Italy for **Conran's,** the Basics Trolley is compact enough (25½ inches high by 16 wide and 10½ deep) to be tucked neatly out of the way until it's needed. Its three plastic-coated wire shelves will give you lots of room to organize pots and pans, garden or household tools, laundry supplies, or other items you'd rather not give valuable shelf space in the kitchen or pantry. Available in red or white, the trolley rolls easily on four metal casters, so even heavy equipment can be moved with minimum effort.

CONTAINERS. Among the practical accessories **Placewares** features in its catalogue and at its stores are many versatile stacking baskets and drawers (*right*) that can solve just about any storage problem. The plastic utility baskets shown at upper right are ingeniously designed to stack if turned in one direction; if you want to store a group of them, simply reverse them to form a compact nest that won't usurp much room in a closet. Stacking bins with ventilation holes can help preserve root vegetables such as onions and potatoes, or you might put some in a closet or along the walls of a child's room to hold clothes and toys.

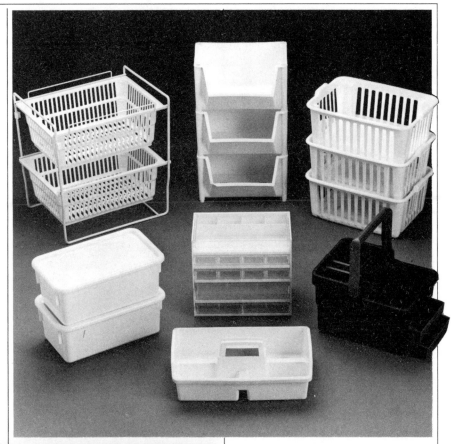

MORE CONTAINERS. Whether you need to reorganize the cabinet under the kitchen sink or want to bring some order to the front hall closet, **Placewares** has a container system that will probably be just right. Many of its modular storage units are made of brightly colored plastic (red, yellow, and blue are often available in addition to white) that will add a cheerful note to a dark corner. Casters can be added to some of the components if you need extra mobility.

ELFA PANTRY. If your kitchen doesn't have a spacious pantry where you can store bulky canned goods, cereals, and the like, why not make one using Elfa components chosen from **Place-wares** or **Lynk** to fit the space? Both shelves and drawers (*below*) slide out easily on wide tracks, and the open design lets you see where everything is located, saving valuable time when you're pulling together all the ingredients for a favorite recipe or four-course dinner.

ELFA STORAGE SYSTEM. Because it consists of a number of modular components that can be fitted together in many different con-figurations, the Elfa system from **Lynk** and **Placewares** (*above*) can provide extra storage in any out-of-the-way area, no matter how confined or oddly shaped. Drawers range from 3⅜ to 14½ inches high and from 9 to 20¾ inches wide (standard depth is 20¾ inches).

LYNK

Both a manufacturer and an importer of shelving systems, Lynk offers a wide range of models that can be tailored to fit almost any storage requirements. One of its imports from Scandinavia is the Elfa system featured here. Another (*not shown*), is Skanshelf modular wood shelving, whose more than 160 com-ponents can be set up in various con-figurations to form extra closets, cabinets, utility storage—and even beds and tables.

Hanging Racks and Utility Shelving

If you've reorganized all of your closets and cabinets, thrown away the items you never use, and installed some modular shelves to help contain the clutter, you may still find that you don't have enough storage room. If so, consider using a wall, the back of a closet door, or the underside of a kitchen cabinet to accommodate some of the items that won't fit anywhere else. There are innumerable wall racks and utility shelves available in sizes appropriate for just about any location you might have in mind. If you are faced with the problem of finding a place to store garden or household tools or outdoor games, there are wall racks designed for the purpose that will keep the portable grill, rake, shovel, badminton set, hose, saw, and stepladder neatly organized on a convenient wall. Just a few of the many options to be considered are featured on the following pages.

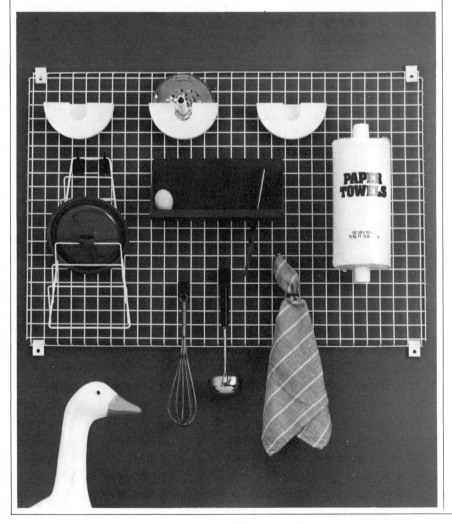

CLOTHES HAMPER. If you have to deal with a tiny bathroom that has no space for a freestanding hamper, why not hang one on the back of the door? **Thonet**'s chrome-plated steel basket is 18 inches high, 12″ wide, and 8″ deep. It is specially made to fit within a Thonet wardrobe (see page 118), but one like it could serve just as well in another location. You could even use it as a convenient hanging wastebasket by adding a paper or plastic liner.

HELLER GRIDS. Vinyl-coated wire wall grids are offered by **Placewares** in three sizes, ranging from 12 by 24½ inches to 25½ by 37½ inches. Once you've picked the right size and color (red, white, or black), clip on the special nylon hooks, which can hold matching wire baskets (also offered in three sizes), a paper towel holder, or your own kitchen utensils, oven mitts, and other household gadgets.

STOR-RACK. Because of its compact design (each unit is only 4¾ inches deep), you could attach one of these hanging racks (*above*) to the back of a kitchen cabinet or vanity door, or arrange several on the wall in a stairwell or narrow hallway. **Schulte Corporation** makes its Stor-rack available in two- , three- and four-shelf models, each of which comes in three widths, for a total of nine separate options. The Stor-rack is made of white epoxy-coated steel rod shelving strong enough to support heavy items with ease.

DOR-WALL RACK. Designed in a 77-inch length to fit any standard door, **Schulte**'s Dor-wall rack is less than 5 inches deep—narrow enough so that it won't prevent the door from closing properly, but big enough to accommodate economy-size cans of juice, fruit, and vegetables. (It is shown here as an adjunct to one of Schulte's installed shelving systems.) You might want to order several extra racks to augment utility storage on a workshop or laundry-room wall. Available in three widths (12, 18, and 24 inches), the rack is made from a one-piece unit of welded steel with a bonded epoxy coating that eliminates sharp edges and is easy to clean.

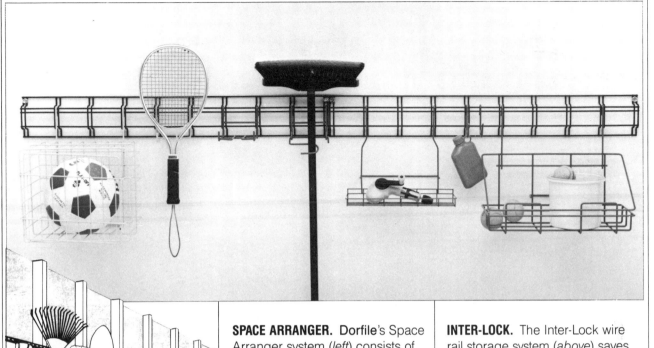

SPACE ARRANGER. Dorfile's Space Arranger system (*left*) consists of 32- or 48-inch steel bars that can be hung from any wall, using the screws provided (or masonry anchors if needed). Once you have positioned the bars in a configuration that suits the tools you want to store, select a hook appropriate for each tool (from a garden hose to a rake, shovel, or bicycle) and snap them in place. The hooks can be rearranged whenever necessary without rehanging the supporting bars.

STORE MORE. The Store More closet system (see page 114) is versatile enough to use in a laundry room or workshop that needs some organization. As shown at left, any of the modular pieces can be mounted high on a wall to provide additional storage space out of the line of traffic. All components slide together to create a solid cabinet; the quick-locking assembly patented by **Alumax** eliminates the need for separate hardware.

INTER-LOCK. The Inter-Lock wire rail storage system (*above*) saves space by organizing and hanging things out of the way, yet keeping them visible for easy access. The mounting rails are available in 24-, 36-, and 48-inch lengths. Matching accessories offered by **Placewares** include six hook designs, a hose hanger, a special holder for footballs or basketballs, several baskets, and a utility shelf. An especially thoughtful feature is a storage cabinet that you can padlock to keep harmful sprays and detergents away from curious children. All components are made of heavy-gauge steel with an epoxy coating in white, red, or black.

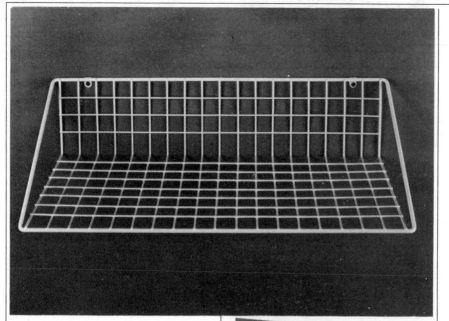

ROVEL UTILITY SHELF. Rovel's compact utility shelf would be equally useful in the bathroom, kitchen, or workroom as an extra place to hold anything from towels and toys to small appliances. Constructed of vinyl-covered steel wire, the shelf is available in white, black, or red and is offered in two sizes (8½ by 15 inches and 11 by 24 inches). **Better Houseware Corp.** includes the screws and anchors necessary for easy installation.

BETTER HOUSEWARE CORP.

Whether you need a set of vinyl-coated wire shelves to augment your cupboard space, a bathroom shower rack to hold your shampoo and bubble bath, a cake rack, or a cookie cutter, chances are Better Houseware Corp. makes it. The New York City manufacturer, founded in 1939, specializes in all sorts of hard-to-find kitchen utensils; under its subsidiary, Rovel, it produces utility shelving, trolleys, and grid systems. While the company does not sell direct to the consumer, its products are at Bon Marché and other stores throughout North America. (Should you have difficulty locating a particular item, Better Houseware will be happy to suggest an appropriate local dealer.)

ROVEL GRID SYSTEM. The difference between Rovel's grid system and others available is that Rovel's comes complete with three accessories: a basket and a shelf that hook onto the grid, and an oval basket that attaches by means of separate grid hooks. **Better Houseware Corp.** makes the vinyl-coated steel-wire grids (not shown) in white, black, or red, and in three sizes: 12 by 18, 18 by 24, and 24 by 36 inches.

CLOSET MAID LINEN/PANTRY UNIT.
One of the newest designs offered by **Clairson International**, the Closet Maid linen or pantry storage unit requires less installation time than a fixed system, yet offers equal versatility. The shelves are held in place by rear poles that attach to the wall with sturdy endcaps and a center bracket. Once the back poles are attached, various widths of shelving and drawers quickly clip into the brackets on 84-inch tall rear and front poles. You can choose drawers for a pantry, flat shelves for a linen or clothes closet, or a combination of the two. All necessary hardware is included.

ROSTI UNDER-CABINET RACK.
If you find that the clutter on your kitchen counter is usurping most of your work space, think about moving some of the staples up out of the way with a new set of containers and a clever under-cabinet rack to hold them. **Placewares** stocks both the Rosti rack and the canisters that slip into it. Airtight lids are available in white, yellow, red, or blue; the clear plastic canisters come in six different sizes.

VENTAIRE DOOR/WALL RACK.
Ventaire door and wall racks are available in a wide range of sizes and models suitable for any number of uses. There are a fixed rack with two, three, four, or eight shelves, and an adjustable two-shelf rack that can easily handle the tallest cans and bottles you need to store. (Several adjustable racks can be positioned one above the other for extra shelf space.) **Dorfile** offers its Ventaire racks in either white or brown vinyl-coated steel; all necessary hardware is included.

STOR-UP SHELVING. There are a number of places in any home where this ingenious shelving design could be put to good use. You might put a unit in a closet, where it would be accessible when needed but unobtrusive when not. Or mount one on the wall of a cluttered garage to add work space for special projects. Or hang one next to the washer and dryer, where the shelves will be available to hold clean laundry as you fold it. **Quaker Industries** manufactures both the three- and four-tier models of heavy-gauge steel with a durable beige coating; all shelves measure a generous 15 inches wide by 14 deep. The larger model can be ordered with twin clothes hangers and a detachable wire basket, each of which will remain in an upright position even when the unit is folded.

CHAPTER 8

Children's Furnishings

Beds

·

*Storage and
Accessories*

Children's Furnishings

A newborn's needs are simple ones: nourishment, a few tiny layettes, a basinette, and a regular change of disposable diapers will serve very well for the first few months of life—along with lots of tender care, of course. Yet as a baby grows, so do the number of objects necessary to both its physical and emotional welfare. Everything from the bed to the storage pieces to the chairs will have to change as the child matures. If your budget won't be stretched to the breaking point by replacing most of the child's furniture several times during the stages of his life, you can start with a crib and a changing table, then trade them in for a toddler bed and a few drawers, and finally bring in an adult-size bed, bureaus, a desk, and bookshelves when homework becomes a nightly event. For those of us who don't have unlimited capital, however, there are alternatives— furniture selections flexible enough to grow with the child or children who will be using them.

Among the most ingenious designs offered by children's furniture manufacturers today are beds engineered to grow from toddler size to adult length simply by adding an extra section of mattress. More commonly available are sturdily made, well designed bunks that offer sleeping room for two children (or even three, with the addition of a trundle), and can be taken apart to use as twin beds when the kids are ready for a more sophisticated look. High trundle beds can be

even more flexible: some contain lots of storage beneath, including desks that can be pulled out when it's time to do the math assignment. Such pieces can be especially helpful when more than one child has to share a cramped room.

Children's needs for adequate storage space to hold treasures and clothes are no less important than those of adults. Surely one of the admonishments most often passed from parent to child is some variation on the theme, "clean up your room." While it is certainly a good idea for children to learn how to organize their belongings, this responsibility can be made more fun than work if the storage components are specifically designed with a child in mind. Brightly colored cubes can hold toys and books just as easily as standard shelves; canvas wall pockets can help to keep socks and underwear in good order. Both are not only practical, but provide imaginative decorations, as well. Modular storage systems can be augmented as required to hold both a toddler's games and an adolescent's record collection. There are even freestanding closet systems, made with children in mind, with clothes rods just the right height for tiny hands to reach.

When it comes to providing flexible children's furniture, contemporary designers have not neglected any basic items—even chairs are made to be useful through several stages of a child's growth. One particularly ingenious model is a toddler's armchair that can be used at three different heights merely by flipping it over to a different position. Another is a highchair that becomes a desk and chair just the right size for a kindergartner.

All of the children's furnishings presented in this chapter, no matter their style, materials, or function, share one common feature: they are designed to withstand years of the kind of abuse only children can dish out.

Beds

When it comes to choosing a bed for a child, you will probably be looking for a piece of furniture that is as rugged as it is comfortable. And unless money is no option, you'll want to select a style that will still be appropriate when your toddler becomes an adolescent. Another consideration, whether or not you plan to enlarge your family, might be to provide room for the small guest who is sure to be invited to stay occasionally. Yet since your child's room is probably the smallest bedroom in your home, you may have to choose a bed or set of beds that won't usurp too much space. Bunks are one option, of course, and there are many models to choose from, just a few of which are featured on these pages. But there are other possibilities, including trundles and loft beds ingeniously designed to take up a minimum amount of the floor area that should be left free for other activities.

CHILDSPACE. All of the modular components of **H.U.D.D.L.E.**'s Childspace series can be assembled using only a screwdriver, an Allen wrench, and instructions supplied by the company. Pieces are finished in white or blue lacquer (bed rails and drawer fronts are offered in solid pine); all are coated with durable, scratch-resistant polyurethane. Choose a corner bunk arrangement (as shown), twin beds, or separate bunks, and then add matching storage pieces—shelves, desks, bureaus, and wardrobes among them.

BIG TOOBS. Designed to encourage a child's imagination as well as to provide a secure place to sleep, Big Toobs are cylinders of molded plywood brightly laminated in a tough vinyl coating that can take lots of abuse. H.U.D.D.L.E. offers the Toobs in a rainbow of cheerful colors, including red, blue, yellow, green, orange, and white. The beds can be stacked or used singly; match or contrast them with tubular bookcases, tables, and stools to create an environment that is as charming as it is practical.

H.U.D.D.L.E.

H.U.D.D.L.E. is the acronym for "Hull Urban Design Development Laboratory, Etcetera", founded in 1970 by a team of specialists with backgrounds in architecture, urban design, and elementary education. Their goal was to research, design, and manufacture furnishings specifically geared for changing modern lifestyles. Many of the company's designs, therefore, are modular groupings or individual pieces that can be expanded as the family—or the child—grows. Colors and shapes are employed with great flair and originality; each item is carefully tested to make sure it can endure rough handling in even the most active household.

VAR BEDS. The practical Var design (*left*) offers plenty of options for a growing family. You might begin with a pair of bunks (guard rail and ladder included) and add two capacious storage drawers on wheels to slip beneath the lower one. As the children mature, the bunks can be taken apart to use as twin beds (and even moved to separate rooms). With the addition of a pair of bolsters, each can be easily transformed into a sophisticated daybed. If you need space for a third child, you might want to replace the storage drawers with a matching trundle. **The Children's Room** offers the Var series in teak, polished pine, or oak.

JGM TRUNDLE. Part of an entire line of furnishings from **The Children's Room** that is notable for its clean, spare design and bright white lamination, the JGM Trundle bed (*right*) slips under a single bed or can be used beneath a matching loft bed or pair of bunks. Because it is not connected to any other bed, it can be used on an opposite wall—or even in another room. The trundle rolls out easily on casters, so even a young child can help make up the bed for an overnight guest.

QUATRAIN HIGH SLEEPER. An excellent choice for a tiny cubicle, the Quatrain High Sleeper measures only 43 inches high by 39 wide and is 76¾ inches long. Within those compact dimensions, however, are a twin bed, a pull-out desk, two bookcases, and a set of drawers. (You might put a pair of the sleepers in a cramped room that has to be shared by two growing children.) Made in Denmark of solid pine and pine veneer, the Quatrain is shipped knocked down by **Conran's,** which provides comprehensive instructions for quick assembly.

TRUNDLE/BED. Made of solid pine, and constructed to withstand the bombardment of children, pets, and slumber parties, this durable bed from the **Pine Factory** is designed to be used singly, or to be stacked one on top of another to form space-saving bunks. Either a matching trundle or a pair of storage drawers can be placed beneath the bed.

PINE BUNKS. One of the problems inherent in some bunk beds is their length, which may be generous enough for a pre-teen, but not for a six-foot adolescent who is trying out for the basketball team. **Conran's** offers solid pine beds that are each a full 80 inches long, offering ample head and foot room for most growing children. The beds can be ordered separately, or you might opt for a pair that can be used as bunks with the addition of connectors, a security bar, and a ladder—all available in an optional package.

TEEN BED. Storage drawers beneath and an attached bookcase/headboard at one end make the **Door Store**'s single bed an especially practical idea for an adolescent's room. Available in bright white with contrasting red drawer pulls, or in teak veneer, the bed can be ordered with matching four- and six-drawer chests, as shown; you might add the Door Store's well-designed student desk to provide work space, extra drawers, and a three-tier bookshelf.

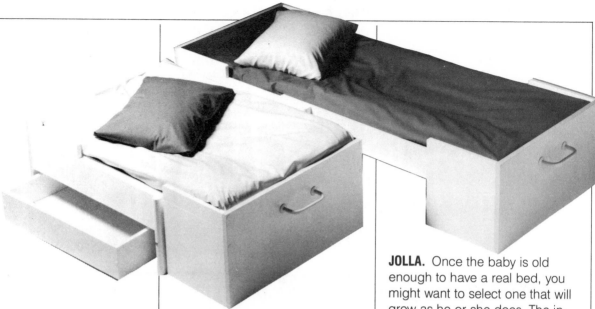

JGM LOFT HOUSE. One of many styles available in the JGM line from **The Children's Room,** the loft bed (*below*) is 45 inches tall, providing ample space for toddlers to play beneath. (There would also be room for an extra bed to be moved part of the way under it in an "L" shape, if you prefer.) Finished in white with birch edges, the JGM loft sports rungs and supports in bright red or white. Matching bookcases, chests, or a wardrobe (as shown) can square off the end of the loft. If you need to fit two beds in a confined space, you can choose the same style as a set of bunks.

JOLLA. Once the baby is old enough to have a real bed, you might want to select one that will grow as he or she does. The ingenious Jolla expands from slightly over crib size to adult length simply by pulling the ends apart and adding the extra mattress section included. **The Children's Room** offers the Jolla in white with birch edges; it expands from 33 by 53 inches to 33 by 77 inches, and has a convenient storage drawer beneath.

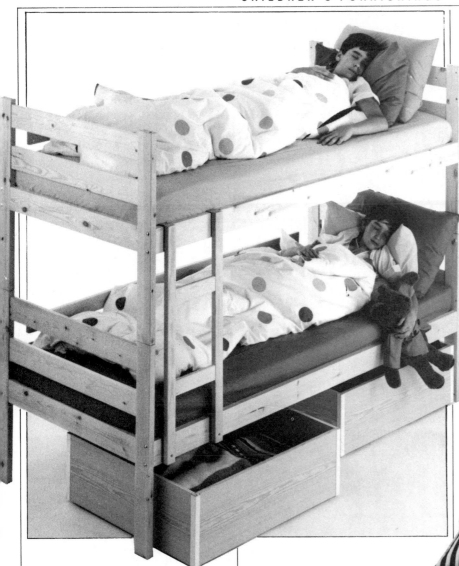

REKO BUNKS. Two ample storage boxes on casters (*left*) are designed to fit beneath the bottom Reko bunk to provide a place for toys, games, and clothing. Made of clear lacquered pine, the bunks measure 34¼ inches wide by 79½ inches in length. They can be stacked, as shown, or used separately (the ladder is optional). **Ikea** supplies the Reko bunks and several other styles knocked down; complete instructions are included, and assembly takes only minutes.

WITT BED. Designed by Knut Hagberg and Marianne Hagberg, the Witt (*right*) is a minimally styled single bed finished in white lacquer. The optional trundle is fitted with casters, so it will roll out easily whenever needed. **Ikea** supplies both bed and trundle knocked down for quick assembly at home; mattresses are offered separately.

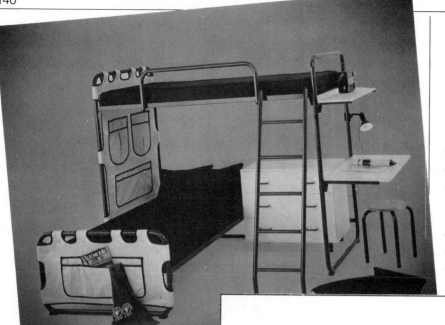

BUNK BEDS. Shown at left in an L-shaped configuration, **Amisco**'s bunk beds can also be stacked atop each other if space is at a premium. (If you need additional sleeping area, you could fit a matching trundle under the bottom bunk). A handy work table can be attached to the side bars, as can a shelf to hold books or a reading light. The steel-tubing beds can be finished in your choice of bright epoxy colors and are shipped knocked down for assembly at home.

AMISCO

Amisco specializes in home furnishings constructed of steel tubing, a material which it forms in sinuous configurations and finishes in a variety of lively colors. Among the company's many offerings for children are cribs, full-size beds, and a group of accessories all characterized by their durability and practicality. Many of the pieces can be rearranged as a child grows—bunks can become twin beds, single beds can be turned into more sophisticated daybeds, and accessories can be added as necessary to provide places for homework as well as for play. The clever "dumping bags" supplied by Amisco (*shown above*) are made of cotton canvas with red, blue, or yellow piping. Snapped on to the bed rails, they would provide an incentive for even the most recalcitrant child to keep things tidy.

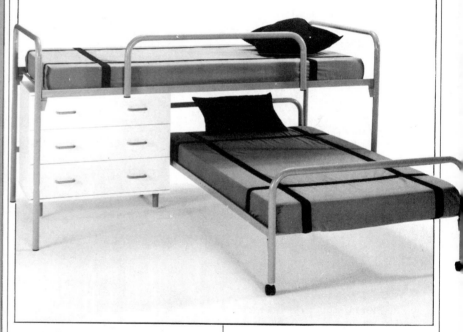

CONDO BEDS. The lower of **Amisco**'s two Condo beds is fitted with casters which enable it to be pulled out effortlessly whenever needed (the upper can be supplied with them at your option). A three-drawer dresser (finished in beige, white, gray, or black) can be attached to the upper bed; drawer pulls can be ordered in a matching or contrasting color. Amisco offers the steel-tubing beds in a rainbow of epoxy finishes: among the choices are red, peach, pink, yellow, navy blue, and brown. Mattresses are not included.

Storage and Accessories

As children mature, so do the number of possessions they accumulate and the number of activities they participate in. The baby's crib and a couple of drawers to hold the layettes give way to the preschooler's books and games and the ten-year-old's needs for a quiet place to do homework and a more capacious area to store the ever-burgeoning wardrobe. Thoughtfully designed storage pieces and accessories can be adapted as your child grows, and thus remain as suitable for the teenager's record and tape collection as they were for the toddler's dolls and train sets. Manufacturers who specialize in children's furnishings can even provide chairs whose seat heights can be adjusted to accommodate growing youngsters.

SINGLE-ROD TWIN ORGANIZER. A pair of 36-inch stacking cabinets from the **Alumax** closet system can be fitted with an expandable clothes rod between them to create a storage area just the right size for a toddler to reach. The cabinets are finished in a beige or oak veneer; you might want to stain or paint them in a color that will complement the decor of your child's room.

TRIPP TRAPP. The Scandinavians can usually be depended upon to create designs which are as clever as they are useful. **Westnofa**'s Tripp Trapp, designed by Peter Opsvik, can be used as a high chair (*below, far right*) or can be transformed at whim to a step stool or a chair for a toddler or an adult; all you have to do is to change the positions of the two horizontal wood pieces. Westnofa can finish the chair in your choice of colorful laminates or in a clear varnish that will bring out the natural wood grain.

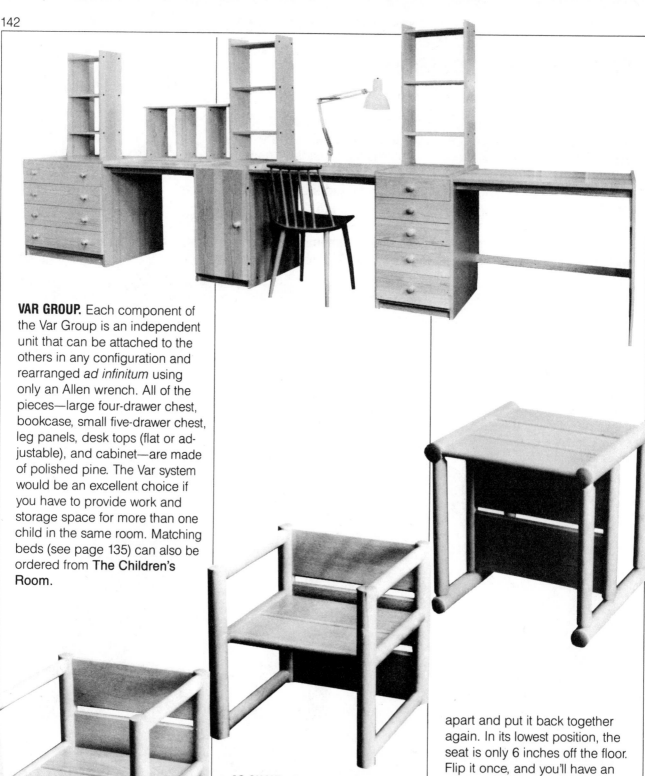

VAR GROUP. Each component of the Var Group is an independent unit that can be attached to the others in any configuration and rearranged *ad infinitum* using only an Allen wrench. All of the pieces—large four-drawer chest, bookcase, small five-drawer chest, leg panels, desk tops (flat or adjustable), and cabinet—are made of polished pine. The Var system would be an excellent choice if you have to provide work and storage space for more than one child in the same room. Matching beds (see page 135) can also be ordered from **The Children's Room**.

AG CHAIR. As your child grows, this cleverly designed chair can be used at three different seat heights simply by flipping it over—there is no need to take it apart and put it back together again. In its lowest position, the seat is only 6 inches off the floor. Flip it once, and you'll have an armchair with a 7½-inch-high seat; once again, and it becomes a stool with a seat height of 12½ inches. **The Children's Room** offers the AG chair in solid beech.

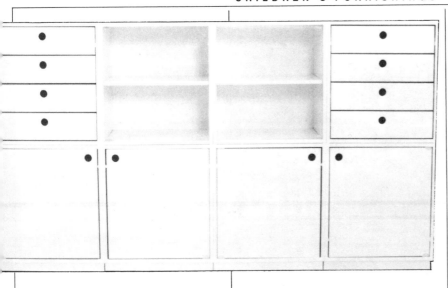

VI DESK. The top of the VI Desk is designed as a separate unit that can be placed with its vertical support either to the left or right of the four-drawer pedestal. And because it isn't permanently fixed, it can be moved out easily to create more work space and knee room, but slid back flush with the pedestal after the homework is finished. **The Children's Room** offers the desk in either teak or oak. Its oak swivel chair has a fully adjustable seat and back that can be raised as a child grows (the seat height ranges from 15 to 21 inches).

KAS CUBES. Modular cube systems provide flexible storage for growing youngsters. It's not difficult or expensive to augment the number of cubes as a child's collection of belongings increases, and they can be placed in various arrangements depending on the space available. Each Kas cube can be set on a 2″-base to raise it slightly off the floor. Both cabinet and bookshelf components feature single adjustable shelves; the bureau unit has four drawers. **The Children's Room** offers the cubes in all-white laminate or in white with birch doors and birch drawers.

THE CHILDREN'S ROOM

The Children's Room was launched in 1970 with the intention of finding new sources of children's furniture and bringing to North America items that had not been available before. In its search for quality furnishings, the company avoids designs that are trendy and easily outmoded, concentrating instead on classic styles, good construction, and reasonable prices. Many of the pieces featured in its catalogue and retail store are imported from Scandinavia. Although The Children's Room is based in New York City, it maintains an efficient mail-order service to reach customers in all parts of North America.

GEMS. Made of rugged canvas with a plastic-coated back, the Gems hanging storage unit has six handy pockets to keep games, books, magazines, and even clothes in apple-pie order. Inexpensive enough so that you might want to cover an entire wall with them, Gems is offered by **Ikea** in bright red canvas with bold black numerals.

CUBES. Brightly colored plastic cubes can be stacked on their sides to make a wall of storage units or a bookcase, or used independently to stash a few treasures. Offered by the **Door Store** in red, yellow, blue, white, and brown, the cubes could be just the right incentive for children not otherwise inclined to organize their belongings and are portable enough for even a toddler to maneuver.

FOLDING STOOL. Available in two sizes (with a seat height of 18 or 24 inches and an overall height of 26 or 33 inches), **Amisco**'s folding stool is made of one-inch steel tubing with a hardwood seat. The frame can be epoxied in green, red, yellow, white, or black to match Amisco's bunks or condo beds (see page 140). The higher stool could be used by a toddler not quite tall enough to sit comfortably at the dining room table; either size folds compactly so that it can be stashed out of the way when not required.

BABUIN. At first glance, the Babuin might appear to be a standard high chair—certainly a useful item for a small child, but not an extraordinary one. Yet by taking the detachable seat out of the frame, laying the frame on its side, and placing the seat in a different location on the frame, the Babuin becomes a small table with a seat attached—perfect for a toddler who needs a place to use paper and crayons. In addition, the seat can be adapted for use as a baby swing by adding four optional ropes; a fitted cushion is available to support tiny tushies. **Ikea** makes the Babuin in bright yellow epoxy-lacquered steel tubing with a plastic seat and fiberboard table top.

STUDENT DESK AND CHAIR. A folding writing desk made of ash wood is offered by **Placewares** with a white or black melamine top or in multicolored dyes of red, black, and yellow. The matching folding chair is available with a solid or lattice-work seat. The desk top is a spacious 38½ inches wide by 23⅝ deep— enough to hold several textbooks and a notepad and still leave room for adolescent elbows.

STOR-DRAWER SYSTEM. Modular steel-mesh baskets coated with white or brown epoxy offer lots of storage options. The frames to hold the baskets are offered by **Schulte** in sizes ranging from 17¾ to 40⅝ inches high and from 12¾ to 20¾ inches wide. Baskets come in depths from 3¼ to 11¾ inches. You can add flat shelves, solid tops, and shoe shelves. While the Stor-Drawer system would fit in a closet, it might also make sense kept out in the open as a reminder to a disorganized child that there can be, in fact, a place for everything.

CHAPTER 9

Outdoor Furniture

*Chairs and
Chaise Longues*

·

Tables and Trolleys

Outdoor Furniture

Among the most pleasant places to relax on a steamy August afternoon is the broad, sheltered veranda of an old-fashioned house. Such an idyllic location calls for the appropriate furnishings: wicker or wrought-iron tables to hold a pitcher of lemonade or iced tea, and well-cushioned chairs in which to laze while sipping a cool drink. Yet the generously proportioned furniture suitable for a wide Victorian porch would look totally out of place on the narrow balcony or pocket-handkerchief patio which is often the only outdoor living area appended to a contemporary home or apartment. If your outdoor space is limited, you'll want to choose furnishings that are in proper scale. Moreover, if you don't have a capacious lawn or patio, your corresponding storage room—in a garage, basement, or garden shed—may be equally limited, making it difficult to store summer furnishings at the end of the season. And if you haven't even a sliver of lawn or porch to call your own, you'll be looking for light, portable chairs that you can carry with you to the beach or the park and tuck away in a closet when you get home.

No matter your reasons for selecting portable summer furniture, you needn't settle for dime-a-dozen aluminum and webbing chairs and fake veneer folding tables that must be whisked under cover at the merest hint of rain. Contemporary manufacturers are employing space-age materials in the construction of stylish, comfortable furnishings that can be left out on the lawn or patio all summer long without detriment. Occasional grime or the residue from an errant flock of birds can be removed with a spray from the garden hose. Chairs and tables available today are durable enough to withstand the onslaught of legions of summer visitors, yet light enough to move around from one location to another whenever the mood strikes. Some of the pieces are even good-looking enough to use indoors—a special benefit if your budget is as tiny as your balcony.

What these furnishings all have in common is their portability: roomy armchairs are designed to stack or to fold so that a number can be stored in a very tight space. Practical serving trolleys feature removable shelves that double as serving trays. Spacious tables that fold compactly for storage include built-in handles to make them easy to tote around; smaller occasional tables, when folded, can be hung from a convenient wall.

Any of the pieces featured on the following pages will serve admirably, so once you've made a selection that suits your particular lifestyle, you'll have no excuse not to dust off the hibachi or grill and invite the hordes for an afternoon feast.

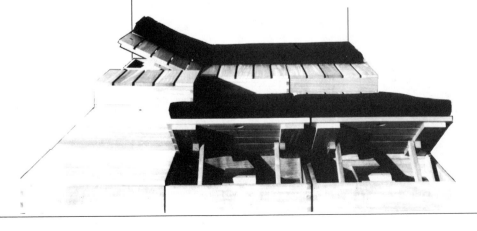

Chairs and Chaise Longues

The basic problem with a lot of so-called "outdoor furniture" is that it isn't really weatherproof. Aluminum chairs with webbed seats and backs tend to rust in spots; the webbing will rot after a few seasons of use. So although such chairs are portable from the standpoint of both their light weight and their capacity to fold, they aren't necessarily good choices for porch or patio. Contemporary manufacturers are providing other options which are as handsome as they are practical. Many of their chairs are finished in space-age materials that are just about impervious to Mother Nature's capriciousness, even if she is abetted by man's soot- and smog-filled city air. Most of the chairs featured here can be left out with impunity in all weather; you can clean them easily with a garden hose and a soapy sponge from time to time. When summer is over, they will fold, or stack in neat piles, to be put away without displacing too much precious storage space.

RIO. Strong but lightweight steel grids form the seat and back of the **Door Store**'s Rio; steel tubing, the arms and legs. Completely coated with an easy-to-clean white polyvinyl, the chair stacks high for storage. Offered in either a high- or low-back style as you prefer, Rio can be fitted with optional cushions for extra comfort.

COTTON SLING. The brightly colored seaside motifs printed on the **Door Store**'s cheerful beach chair might convince you you're at the shore even if you are only sunning yourself on a city rooftop. Four separate patterns are available, each printed on cotton canvas attached to a natural wood frame. The back of the chair can be adjusted to any one of four positions. When you have had enough sun, the chair folds to a sliver for storage.

FIESTA. Whether you're off for a day at the beach, a weekend in the country, or an *al fresco* lunch in the park, you might want to bring a couple of the **Door Store**'s Fiesta chairs along. Made of candy-striped nylon canvas slung over a white-finished steel frame, they weigh almost nothing and fold compactly enough to be tossed in the trunk or tucked under an arm. If the residue of too many picnics becomes evident, the sling can always be removed and tossed in the washing machine.

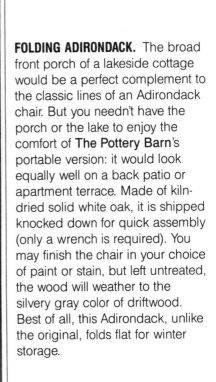

FOLDING ADIRONDACK. The broad front porch of a lakeside cottage would be a perfect complement to the classic lines of an Adirondack chair. But you needn't have the porch or the lake to enjoy the comfort of **The Pottery Barn**'s portable version: it would look equally well on a back patio or apartment terrace. Made of kiln-dried solid white oak, it is shipped knocked down for quick assembly (only a wrench is required). You may finish the chair in your choice of paint or stain, but left untreated, the wood will weather to the silvery gray color of driftwood. Best of all, this Adirondack, unlike the original, folds flat for winter storage.

BELMAR. The Belmar armchair is made of aluminum coated with a smooth acrylic finish available in thirteen colors, including a choice of greens, daffodil yellow, white, brown, orange, and terra cotta. The result is an eminently practical chair that won't snag clothing or rust. **Molla** makes the chair and a matching chaise longue (not shown) of aluminum, a material that is light in weight but strong enough to handle years of abuse and all kinds of weather conditions. (The lounge is offered with or without custom-fitted cushions in a range of patterns and complementary colors.) Both chair and chaise will stack easily when it's time to put them away.

MOLLA, INC.

In its Westbury, New York, factory, Molla produces a wide range of cast aluminum outdoor furniture under the registered trademark "Alumaloy". Its catalogue features models and designs to suit every preference, from sleek contemporary styles to ornate, detailed Victorian ones. A number of Molla's chairs and chaise longues are available with detachable cushions; others feature webbed strapping instead of aluminum mesh for extra comfort. Many of the company's offerings are designed to be portable: they can be stacked or folded for storage in a minimum amount of space.

FLEXIBLE 3-D DECKING. While most decks certainly cannot be considered furniture, the ingenious, practical mahogany units available from **C I Designs** are just that, and more. They can be arranged in any number of configurations for seating, storage, and decking. Among the most versatile modules available is a 24½"-square, 5½"-high box seat with a hinged top. As illustrated, several of these placed together not only provide a comfortable lounging area with a back that can be raised and lowered, but offer extra room for storing garden tools and other outdoor necessities. C I has foam cushions to fit, and will cover them in a fabric you specify or supply them with natural canvas zippered covers.

DANISH DIRECTOR'S CHAIRS. The ubiquitous director's chair has come a long way from the movie set. You can now find some version of the classic folding chair in virtually any home furnishings store; even discount outlets often carry a selection, however shoddily made. **Conran's** offers an especially handsome interpretation in natural wood with a wide range of colorful canvas seats and backs. While a group of the chairs would look wonderful arranged on a patio or under a favorite shade tree, they are good-looking enough to function equally well indoors.

PASTOE. Made of high-impact polypropylene that is totally resistant to wear, the Pastoe chair (*right*) is available with or without arms and in various color combinations of seat/back and frame that won't fade when exposed to the sun. Designed by Sebel for the **Norix Group,** the Pastoe is designed to knock down for storage in a minimum area. The matching drum table (48 inches in diameter) is available with or without an umbrella.

INTEGRA. Molded polypropylene is formed into the sleek lines of Sebel's Integra stacking chair. A material impervious to corrosive salt, chlorine, sun, and normal temperature extremes, it is available in a wide range of colors. The Integra is offered by the **Norix Group** either with or without arms. Both versions can be stacked fifteen high without wobbling, and the resulting pile will be only 78 inches tall.

VICARIO. Designed by Vico Magistretti for **Artemide,** the Vicario stacking armchair is molded of the company's patented Reglar material, a reinforced polyester impervious to wear and weather. Vicario's colors—white, green, dark brown, Chinese red, and light gray—are integrated in the polyester rather than applied to it for great resistance to scratching. Each armchair measures 18½ inches wide by 19¾ inches deep and is 29½ inches high.

SELENE. Vico Magistretti's side chair is made of the same practical reinforced polyester as is his Vicario armchair. **Artemide** offers it in colors to match the armchair, or in yellow, blue, or magenta. Both models are sophisticated designs that would look equally well indoors or out. Light in weight yet strong enough to withstand lots of abuse, the Selene measures 18½ inches wide by 19¾ deep and is 29½ inches tall. A number can be stacked compactly for storage.

DABAYA FOLDING CHAIR. If you're planning to have a group of friends in for a barbeque and find that you don't have enough chairs to go around, why not consider adding a group of **Allibert**'s stylish Dabaya chairs to your supply of outdoor furniture? Folded flat, they will take up very little space once the party is over, and they are totally weatherproof, so they won't be ruined if you forget to put them away. Seats are contoured for comfort, but Allibert can supply cushions, if you like.

TANGOR. The back of the Tangor armchair can be adjusted to any one of four positions for lounging; special fitted cushions add extra comfort. The chair comes in white; the cushions, in a choice of five different color combinations (**Allibert** can even supply a matching umbrella). While the Tangor is made of durable synthetic resins that are totally weatherproof, it does fold compactly when you want to put it away.

ALLIBERT

Allibert manufactures a comprehensive line of sophisticated outdoor furniture in its Grenoble factories. Common to all of the company's designs are their unmistakable Continental styling and their practicality: each piece is made of a durable synthetic resin compound that is impervious to the effects of sun, rain, and salt- or chlorine-laden air. The material is easy to maintain: just mild soap and water keeps chairs and tables looking fresh and white, even on a sooty urban terrace.

DALGORIA STACKING ARMCHAIR.

Made of the polypropylene resins that **Allibert** uses for all of its outdoor furnishings, the Dalgoria armchair is molded to fit the body's natural contours. So even if you don't add the optional seat cushion, you'll have a chair that will support you in comfort for hours. Each chair measures a roomy 2 feet in width by 21 inches deep and is 32¾ inches high; a group will stack easily for storage.

DALGORIA ARMCHAIR/OTTOMAN.

Adjust the back of the Dalgoria armchair to its lowest position, add the ottoman, and you have a comfortable lounge perfect for whiling away a hot summer afternoon. **Allibert** can supply

detachable cushions for even greater luxury. When company comes, the ottoman can easily double as a convenient side table to hold drinks and snacks. Rear wheels make the chair easy to move around; the spanking white

resin compound used to make both chair and ottoman insures that they won't rust, stain, yellow, blister, or warp, even if left out all summer.

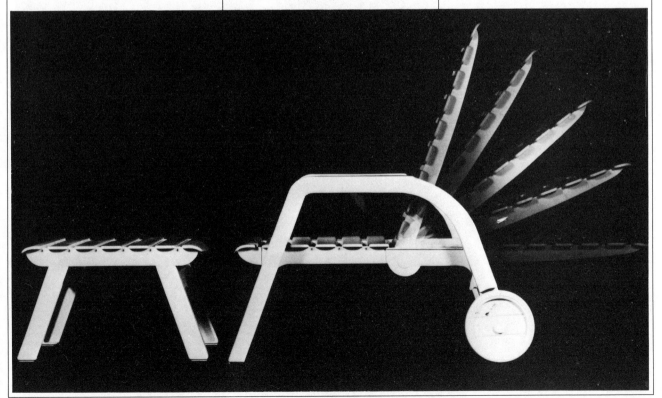

Tables and Trolleys

Even if your back yard is endowed with a handsome redwood picnic table, there will probably be occasions when you'll need some additional tables to hold party snacks and drinks, or to stand next to the grill to keep plates and condiments at hand while the hamburgers and hotdogs sizzle. If your space is limited, you will want to choose occasional tables that can be folded and put away after the guests go home. A number of suitable choices are featured on the following pages. In addition, there are much larger tables that can also be folded when they aren't needed, along with mobile serving carts that can be wheeled effortlessly from one location to another as the situation dictates. All have in common their portability and their imperviousness to weather conditions, so even a passing shower needn't force you to put them away before you're ready to do so.

QUARTINO SERVING CART. The generous size of its wheels and handles makes the Quartino serving cart easy to roll from one location to another; special racks on the bottom shelf will hold bottles securely while the cart is in motion. The trolley, shown with **Allibert**'s Dalgoria stacking armchairs, features drop-leaf sides, so that it won't take up much space until needed for the next cookout or party. One shelf is detachable and becomes a handy extra tray. Allibert includes an umbrella hole as part of the trolley's design, and can supply the umbrella if you need it.

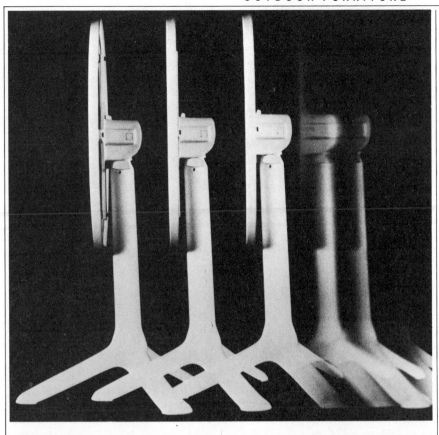

PUB TILT-TOP TABLE. The circular top of the Pub table locks into the vertical position shown for storage; the tripod base provides stability. Available in either a 23- or 32-inch diameter model, the table can be fitted with a patio umbrella. Because the Pub is made of the same durable synthetic resins as **Allibert**'s other outdoor furnishings, it won't be affected by weather or heavy use, and even resists burns and scorching.

TERRACE TABLE. Whether you choose **Allibert**'s Terrace Table in a 42-inch square model or in the rectangular version (42 by 26 inches), you will have an extremely practical outdoor table that can be brought out at a moment's notice to provide lots of room for an impromptu lunch or dinner. But when you don't need it, either size folds to a thickness of only 9 inches for storage. (As you drop the leaves, a hidden handle automatically pops up to make the table easy to carry.) Allibert provides three built-in supports for the addition of one of its umbrellas, eliminating the need for a clumsy, heavy parasol base.

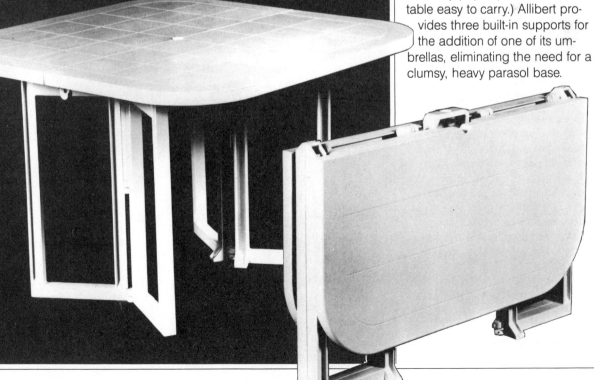

HANG-UP. You'll probably be able to think of lots of occasions when this simple circular table would be a handy adjunct to the other pieces on your porch or patio. **Quaker Industries** makes the 16-inch-diameter table in metal with a baked-on enamel finish in white or beige. It folds easily, and a convenient hook is included, so you can hang it on a wall if you like.

MODEL 13T101. Illustrated here is just one of several square metal folding tables offered by **Quaker Industries.** All are protected from the effects of the weather by a white baked-enamel finish. The model shown measures 17 inches square and the top is made of connecting metal grids. Model 12T100 differs only in size (16 inches square). If you prefer a mesh top, specify model 8T102 (also 16 inches square). If you prefer the look of wood, Quaker makes a redwood-topped folding table (model 20T106) which measures 16 inches square.

QUAKER INDUSTRIES

At its factories in Illinois and in Canada, Quaker Industries manufactures many different types of tables, a number of which are suitable for use indoors or out. In addition to the metal tables and trolleys featured on these two pages, the company offers tray-table sets and other types of occasional pieces, with an emphasis on utility and portability. Most of its designs fold for storage; all of the outdoor furniture is finished in a tough baked enamel coating which is, easy to clean and will withstand occasional showers and extremes of temperature.

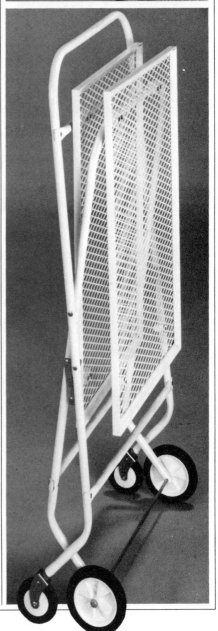

WHITE MESH SERVING CART. Constructed of ⅝-inch tubular steel with a white enamel finish, **Quaker Industries'** handy trolley is designed with utility in mind. As shown at the far right (*top*), both of the 15 by 23-inch shelves are removable so that they can be used as extra trays. (Each is fitted with a security lip to prevent plates and silverware from sliding off.) The back wheels are fixed; the front wheels swivel to make the cart easy to steer. After the party is over, you can fold the trolley without removing the shelves, and it will easily slip into a cramped corner for storage.

BELMAR HOSTESS CART. Each of the removable mesh shelves of **Molla**'s Belmar trolley measures a roomy 18 by 26 inches. The aluminum cart can be finished in any one of thirteen colors to complement or match other pieces in the Belmar collection—nesting tables, stacking chairs, dining tables, and chaises are among the choices offered. All of the furniture is finished in a totally weatherproof acrylic that won't stain, rust, or peel but will clean up easily with soap and water.

CASTELLI TABLE. Injection-molded plastic forms both the top and legs of Kartell's streamlined Castelli table. It can be knocked down for storage and assembles simply by snapping the legs into the top; there are no screws to tighten or metal parts to rust. The table measures 31½ inches square and is 28¼ inches high. Available in white only, it is shown with Kartell's Bartoli chair (in white or red). Both are offered by **Placewares.**

CHAPTER 10

Appliances
and
Accessories

Appliances

·

Kitchen and Bath
Accessories

·

Where to Hide it

·

Where to Hang It

·

The Last Word

Appliances and Accessories

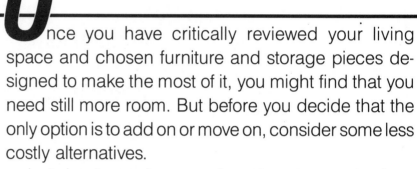

Once you have critically reviewed your living space and chosen furniture and storage pieces designed to make the most of it, you might find that you need still more room. But before you decide that the only option is to add on or move on, consider some less costly alternatives.

Just about every home and apartment, no matter how tiny, comes equipped with a stove and a refrigerator. These two appliances, along with the sink, often take up so much kitchen space that there's little or no room left for counters and cabinets. If your kitchen is a tiny one, you might want to think about replacing the old behemoths that are cramping your style with smaller-scaled, yet equally servicable, appliances such as the ones featured on the next few pages. Should you be faced with creating separate living quarters in your home for another family member out of space that seems less than adequate, a compact, one-piece unit such as those offered by King Refrigerator might fill the bill. Major appliance manufacturers offer scaled-down dishwashers that can be fitted into much less space than their larger cousins, along with the more common portable units that can be rolled up to the sink after dinner, then placed in a corner when not needed. If you are heartily sick

of constant trips to the laundromat and frustrating searches for the right change once you get there, there are washer/dryer units available that can be fitted into a closet or an underutilized corner. (Ingenious designs permit many of the dryers to be installed on an interior wall, as they are self-venting and require no outside connection.)

If there are items you can't put in the dryer, or if you don't *have* a dryer, you might appreciate having a useful laundry rack that fits snugly over the bathtub and collapses neatly once the clothes are dry. An extra towel rack that folds against the wall when it's not in use might also be a handy appurtenance for bath or kitchen, especially when you're expecting overnight guests. And if there isn't sufficient closet space available for your guests' clothes, consider a knock-down valet or clothes tree that can be set up in minutes and stashed away compactly until the next visit.

There are many other accessories, ranging from tools to recreation equipment, that are designed with portability and utility in mind. Folding screens suitable for every decor from Victorian to postmodern can create an instant wall to improve an unwieldy floor plan, hide an unsightly mess, or provide extra privacy. A stepladder that telescopes to a sliver for storage; an ingenious little fan that screws into a common light-bulb socket; even a folding exercise bicycle—these are among the current offerings from manufacturers sensitive to the space crunch that is affecting so many of us.

Appliances

Economic considerations often dictate that we must live in smaller spaces than we would like. Modern kitchens in both houses and apartments tend to be cramped little nooks—afterthoughts in the design of the overall floor plan. It is encouraging to find that major appliance manufacturers are cognizant of the ever-diminishing sizes of the rooms we live in. They are offering compact, well-designed stoves, refrigerators, washing machines, and dryers that utilize a minimum amount of precious space but are nearly as capacious as the full-size models. Small appliances—microwave ovens, food processors, and can openers among them—are being constructed to slip into specially-made under-cabinet racks, freeing the counter space they once usurped for food preparation and other necessary kitchen tasks. Just a few of the ingenious, space-saving appliances now available are featured on these pages.

SUB-COMPACT MICROWAVE OVEN. Only 9½ inches high by 18¾ wide and 13 inches deep, **Whirlpool**'s small-scale microwave oven can be mounted under an overhead cabinet to save valuable counter space (specify the optional mounting kit, MK100). If you want to bring it along on vacation or use it on the patio, the oven can be slipped out of the mounting brackets with little effort. **Magic Chef** offers a similar model, called the Tuckaway (not shown).

CONTEMPO MATE. No expensive plumbing connections are required for **Speed Queen**'s compact washer; it hooks up to a nearby sink. The dryer doesn't need outside venting—another saving, especially if you can only place it by an inside wall or if you rent, rather than own, your home or apartment. The laundry duo takes up just 4⅓ square feet of floor space, yet can handle regular loads of wash with ease. Optional casters make the appliances easy to maneuver.

WHIRLPOOL COMPACT APPLIANCES.
An 18-inch-wide dishwasher might be the solution if your kitchen isn't as roomy as you'd like it to be. Whirlpool's model DU1800XP (shown to the right of the sink) will handle roughly two-thirds the load of a full-size dishwasher—up to eight place-settings of dishes—but takes much less space than its larger cousin. The Thin Twin washer/dryer is only 23⅞ inches wide by 27¼ deep and stands roughly 6 feet high. Other models in the Whirlpool line of washers and dryers can be mounted on the wall or stacked using special kits the company makes available.

MRC-5 REFRIGERATOR. Whether your kitchen is so tiny that you have no room for a standard refrigerator, or you are looking for a second one for a home office, mother-in-law apartment, or family room, **Magic Chef**'s MRC-5 model might fill the bill. It provides 4.8 cubic feet of space and features a full freezer with ice trays, twin see-through crispers, and a dairy door to hold eggs, butter, and cheeses. You can choose a white or walnut finish.

MINI-KITCHEN. In a space that measures only 30½ inches wide by 25½ deep and 67 inches high, **King Refrigerator Corporation** has managed to fit a two-burner stove, a refrigerator, a sink, and an overhead wall oven (either conventional or microwave). The refrigerator provides six cubic feet of space and features a push-button defrost. The Mini-Kitchen is available in either a gas or electric model and in a white, copper, green, beige, or gold finish.

ALL-IN-ONE KITCHEN CENTER. If you can find just 76 inches of wall space, you can install a complete kitchen, including a 4-burner range and oven (electric or gas), a stainless-steel sink with storage underneath, and a 9.2 cubic-foot refrigerator. **King Refrigerator Corporation** offers its All-in-One Kitchen Center in a choice of five colors and can provide optional wall cabinets and a microwave oven (as shown) to match.

KING REFRIGERATOR CORPORATION

King has been making refrigeration equipment for nearly fifty years and offers a variety of compact appliance combinations measuring from 30 to 72 inches in width. One of its most ingenious offerings is Refresh-ade (not shown), a one-piece fixture only 4 feet wide and less than 3 feet tall, which includes a sink, a two-burner range, a refrigerator, storage space, and a wet bar. A hinged lid hides all appurtenances, and the unit is available in a walnut-grain finish that would blend with the decor of the den or family room. (As a safety feature, the burners shut off automatically when the lid is closed.)

MYSON ELECTRIC TOWEL WARMERS.
Among the most sybaritic comforts on a cold winter morning is a warm towel to envelop you when you emerge from the shower. And you needn't cope with expensive installation to enjoy it. Myson electric warmers come in freestanding or wall-mounted models. Both are totally portable and use no more energy than an ordinary light bulb. Available in several sizes from **ARD Custom Kitchens,** the towel racks come in chrome, gold-plated, or polished-brass finish.

HT COMFORT HEATER AND FAN.
When space is limited, it is a relief to find a combination space heater and fan that is not only compact but also stylish and exceptionally practical. The **Krups** HT model can be used on the floor, desk, or table top. Small yet versatile, it has a five-position control and an adjustable stand for directing air flow. In hot weather, the heater can be converted for use as a cooling fan.

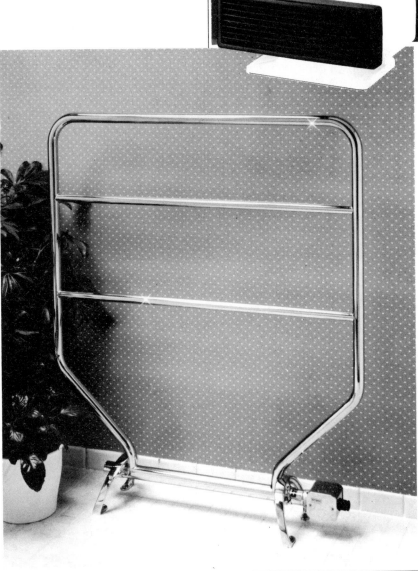

STACK LAUNDRY.
Magic Chef's stack laundry is a full-size laundry system that takes half the normal space. The MDCP-1085 dryer stacks on top of the MWCP-1085 washer, making a perfect space-saving combination for either home or apartment. The Stack Laundry could fit in a closet, as shown, or might slip into an available niche in kitchen or bathroom. In any location, it can handle heavy loads of wash effortlessly, making it a good choice if you must cope with all of the dirty clothes and linens a large family accumulates.

Kitchen and Bath Accessories

Such accoutrements as towel bars and dish drainers that litter the average kitchen and bathroom are generally useful and necessary items. Unfortunately, what they add in utility they generally lack in style. Once you have spent a good deal of effort decorating those two rooms, why spoil the overall effect with ill-designed, cheaply made accessories purchased from the nearest discount store? Especially when there are attractive alternatives available—alternatives which take into account both good looks and utility. Since bathrooms and kitchens are generally among the smallest areas in any home or apartment, space is an important consideration. A drainer that folds to provide additional counter space when the dishes are dry; a towel bar that stores flat against the wall; even a collapsible drying rack for hand washables—these and other accessories can help to make the most of the area you have available.

TOWEL-ON-A-ROPE. The rope and wood-dowel towel holder made by **Better Houseware Corp.** can be hung from any hook, doorknob, or nail, and will hold a roll of paper towels, a pair of hand towels, or two rolls of toilet paper. Perfect for the workshop, kitchen, or bathroom, it is easy to transport from one room to another as required.

FOLDING DISH RACK. The standard dish drainer and ribbed rubber pad that sit beside most kitchen sinks may be useful, but they aren't terribly attractive and are difficult to store when the counter space is needed for other functions. **Better Houseware Corp.** makes a clever folding dish rack that collapses into its own compact case. When open, the interior of the case becomes a drainboard for dripping dishes. The rack holds up to 13 plates, and includes a cutlery holder and grooves to secure cups or glasses. It is available in white, beige, or a combination of red and white.

ADJUSTABLE TOWEL HOLDER. The adjustable stem of **Better Houseware Corp.**'s useful towel holder can be locked in various positions to fit several sizes of paper towels. The holder can be mounted vertically or horizontally on a wall or under a cabinet, or can stand upright on a counter top. It is packed with screws and mounting tape—and even a roll of paper towels.

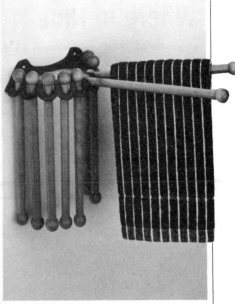

OVER-TUB DRYING RACK. If you don't have room outdoors to hang a clothesline, or if inclement weather spoils your washday plans, you might appreciate **Placewares'** clever drying rack. It will fit any tub, no matter the dimensions, and the mere push of a button will adjust it to one of ten possible flat or angled positions. The metal frame supports a generous 36 feet of plastic-coated line, and the unit folds flat for storage when the laundry is dry.

FOLDING WALL RACK. A reproduction of a design first patented in 1886, **Placewares'** handsome folding wall rack is no less useful today than it was a century ago. An enameled cast-metal holder supports nine fold-down wooden rods to hold utensils, towels, and anything else you want hung within easy reach. The rack is just 7½ inches wide and 11 inches high when folded; the rods extend 13 inches from the wall.

WOODEN DISH RACK. Imported from Sweden by the **Door Store**, this attractive wooden dish rack is stylish enough to leave out for company to admire, but can be folded compactly and stowed under the sink when you need the counter space. You might want to have several extras to keep the dishes inside your cabinets in good order.

Where to Hide It

If you want to partition a studio apartment for privacy, hide an ugly permanent fixture, or temporarily mask the debris in the kitchen from your dinner guests, you needn't resort to an expensive permanent solution such as a new wall or set of sliding doors that require installation. A folding screen can do the trick and add an effective decorative element to the room at the same time. No matter what style, material, or size you select, such a screen can be used in any number of ways. You might make one into an extra "wall" to rearrange an awkward floor plan. A screen made of a transluscent material will block an unattractive view, yet allow natural light to enter your only window. If you move to a new location, or want to make a change in the layout of a room, the screen can be moved to a new spot without effort or folded compactly for storage. Whether you prefer contemporary or period decorating styles, you'll be able to find just the right screen to complement the look you want to create.

SHOJI SCREEN. The frames of the classic Japanese Shoji screen shown above are traditionally made of redwood, but you can have them made of cedar, pine, or basswood if you prefer. **The Shoji Workshop** makes the screens of white translucent fiberglass paper or laminated rice paper. Other fabrics—and glass—are available by special order. The company can supply the tracks and frames to your specifications and will manufacture screens to your precise measurements, whether you want to construct an entire wall or just hide the ugly view from a small window.

JAPANESE SILK SCREEN. The delicately painted silk fireplace screen illustrated below measures three feet in height and is six feet long when fully extended. It is just one of many contemporary Japanese silk screens imported by **The Fran Laufer Collection.** Hand-painted with either floral or court scene motifs, the screens are available in a wide range of sizes and color combinations.

HERRINGBONE. Michael Zevy Berkowicz designed the sleek folding screen shown at left so that its clear acrylic frame and supports are part of the decorative motif. Each panel section is set in separately, so you can specify mirrored acrylic or smoked gray acrylic inserts, or a combination of the two. **Plexability** offers the screen in custom sizes and in other color combinations.

WRIGLEY SCREENS. Cabinetmaker **Rick Wrigley** has collaborated with artist Catherine Creamer on a series of folding screens of unusual quality and good looks. Wrigley is responsible for the fine wood frames; Creamer, for the hand-woven and dyed silk panels. The superb craftsmanship they employ is evident in the detail shown below. Bird's-eye maple predominates in this example, which measures 72 inches high by 80 wide when fully open.

CHARLES EAMES SCREEN. The sinuous lines of this sleek wood screen are composed of laminated ash; canvas inserts between the panels give it flexibility. Created by Charles Eames in 1946, the classic design is available from **Fifty/50,** which specializes in mid-century furnishings and decorative arts.

Where to Hang It

When the closets are crammed to bursting even though you've organized them to a fare-thee-well, why not hang extra garments in plain view? If you choose one of the handsome valets or hangers illustrated on these two pages, the result can be a benefit rather than a liability. If you're having guests on a cold winter evening, you don't have to dump their coats on the bed in an unsightly pile. You might choose, instead, to bring a collapsible coat rack out of the closet and set it up in an alcove or corner. If you choose a design as handsome as the ones featured on these pages, the result will complement your decorating scheme and keep your company's wraps from being crushed.

COAT HANGER. Designed by Roald Steen Hansen and made in Denmark by World Pictures for **The Museum of Modern Art,** this minimally styled laminated beech coat hanger is attached to a wall button fitted with a concealed brass support that attaches easily and firmly to a wall or to the back of a door. Represented in the Museum's design collection, it is a modern classic that provides a convenient place to hang a coat or jacket, and a work of art when unadorned.

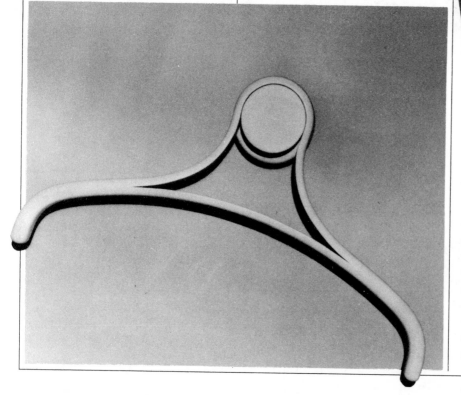

BENTWOOD COAT RACK. Made of either maple or oak, **Curtis Erpelding**'s bentwood coat rack is composed of five sinuous "leaves" that attach to a central core. While the piece is good-looking enough to deserve pride of place in a front hall or entryway, Erpelding has designed it so that it can be knocked down for storage when not needed—after the company goes home, or during the warm summer months when no coats are required.

VALET WITH BENCH. Akko makes its useful valet/bench of half-inch-thick clear or black acrylic (specify model 6158). Extra skirt clips and scarf hooks can be added to your specifications. A convenient shoe bar is affixed to the bottom of the bench; a key shelf and pants rod, to the back. Both the valet/bench and a valet without the bench (model 6150) measure 18 inches wide by 43 inches high. The cushion on the bench model is optional.

SERVETTO. Metal tubing is forced into the whimsical shape of a human figure to form Origlia's ultramodern valet. It can be finished in a choice of neon-bright colors—yellow, pink, blue, green, and red—or in more conservative black, white, or gray. The tubing components slip together easily, so that the valet can be disassembled for storage if you like. The "arm" of the figure swings out 90 degrees from its folded position, providing even more flexibility.

BEDSPREAD HOLDER. There never seems to be enough storage space to hold extra blankets and bedspreads. But if you have a treasured family quilt or fine wool blanket that you reserve for company use, why not keep it on permanent display on Akko's sleek holder? Made of half-inch-thick clear acrylic sturdy enough to support the heaviest spread, it measures 36 inches wide by 34 inches high; the colorless acrylic won't clash with even the brightest spread or Amish quilt.

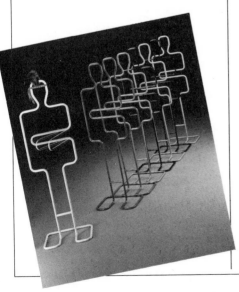

The Last Word

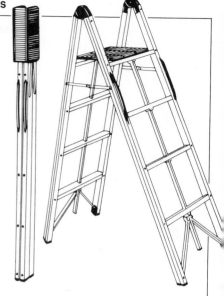

After you have made careful selections of basic fixtures and furnishings to suit your living quarters, no matter how inadequately proportioned they may be, there are some unusual and imaginative accessories that you might want to consider. None of the items featured on these two pages are really essential, yet any of them could add an element of utility or pleasure to your surroundings—and either of those benefits might become an essential in itself. A portable fan, for instance, will stir the air on a hot summer afternoon, while a tromp l'oeil painting could give the impression of a tranquil country vista just outside your window, even if the only real view you have is of a neighboring apartment house wall.

HIDE-A-CYCLE. If you don't think you have sufficient floor space to keep an exercise bike handy, think again. The Hide-a-Cycle, designed by Vitamaster for **Sears**, is made of steel, yet it weighs less than 50 pounds. The seat and legs telescope and the handles fold down, so it can be tucked into a closet after your daily workout. The Hide-a-Cycle is fitted with an odometer so that you can keep track of how many miles you've pedaled.

STEPLADDER. Bon Marché's useful stepladder is standard height and width when open, but it folds to a compact 4¼ by 5½ by 68¾ inches, so that it can be fitted into even the smallest apartment closet. Made of zinc-finished steel coated in red and black, the ladder also comes in a smaller, four-rung model that folds to the same width and depth and is less than five feet high.

NICECOOL FAN. This ingenious little fan (6½ inches long and 7 inches wide) screws into a standard light-bulb socket or can be used in place of track lighting or clip-on lights to provide a refreshing breeze on even the hottest summer days. Offered by **Bon Marché,** the fan is very quiet when operating and uses only 24 watts of power to run.

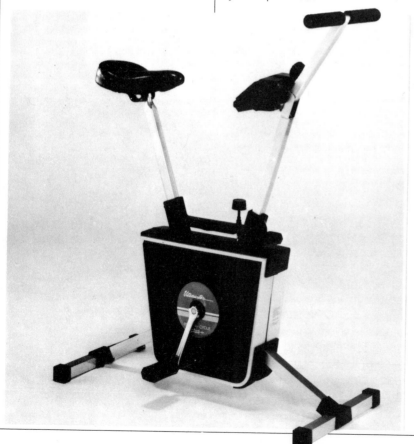

CHINESE DOWRY BASKET. In parts of China, woven reed baskets are given by the prospective groom to the bride's family as a sign of commitment. The baskets are filled with trays of "double happiness" pastries which are passed out to friends and family. **The Fran Laufer Collection** imports the baskets in assorted sizes, patterns, and colors. Each is trimmed with wood and brass and fitted with several deep, removable trays. Because of their flat tops, the baskets can serve as occasional tables and provide extra storage space.

CHICHIBIO. When you need an extra table, why not add your own top to a pair of **Origlia**'s tripod legs? Available in eight lacquer colors or in white maple, they each measure 14¾ inches wide by 28 high when open, and fold flat for storage.

TROMPLOY. When you have tried every possible solution to enlarge your living space and are still feeling cramped, why not hang one of these clever canvas paintings on a wall or over a window that has no view? The artists at **Tromploy** are masters of illusion, and one of their cheerful scenes might just save you from total claustrophobia. Sally Friedman created this particular canvas, which measures 4 by 7 feet; she or one of Tromploy's other artisans can transform a piece of canvas into a tranquil vista of your choosing, or can create visual foolery on a piece of furniture, a folding screen, or a floorcloth, if you prefer.

List of Suppliers

A

Akko Inc.
300 Canal St.
Lawrence, MA 01840
(617) 685-3888

Catalogue available.

Designs and manufactures a wide range of acrylic furniture.

Allibert
119 W. 57th St.
New York, NY 10019
(212) 247-7780

Brochures available.

Imports sophisticated Continental outdoor furniture from its French factory in Grenoble.

Alumax Corporation
P.O. Box 4515
Lancaster, PA 17604
(717) 299-3711

Brochures available.

Offers a wide range of closet and storage systems.

Amisco Industries
CP 250
L'Islet, Que. G0R 2C0
Canada
(418) 247-5025

Brochures available.

Manufactures sleek, sophisticated tubular steel furniture.

Arconas Corp.
580 Orwell St.
Mississauga, Ont. L5A 3V7
Canada
(416) 272-0727

New York Showroom:
150 E. 58th St.
New York, NY 10022
(212) 753-4960

Brochures available.

Manufactures ultramodern home furnishings.

ARD Custom Kitchens and Baths
1 Fourth Pl.
Brooklyn, NY 11231
(718) 624-5688

Brochures available.

Specialists in custom-designed furniture and accessories.

Artemide, Inc.
150 E. 58th St.
New York, NY 10155
(212) 980-0710

Catalogues available.

Trend-setting leader in Italian designs—the latest in contemporary furnishings and fixtures.

Atelier International Ltd.
595 Madison Ave.
New York, NY 10022
(212) 644-0400

Supplies high-quality contemporary furniture.

Axiom Designs
110 Greene St.
New York, NY 10012
(212) 219-2212

Importers of avant-garde Italian furniture.

B

Bedcraft
9123 Lee Hwy.
Fairfax, VA 22031
(703) 698-0100

Brochure available.

Specialists in handcrafted oak platform beds.

Better Houseware Corp.
25-12 41st Ave.
Long Island City, NY 11101
(718) 392-2123

Manufactures kitchen and bath utensils and accessories which it makes available at retail outlets across North America.

Bieffe U.S.A.
227 W. 17th St.
New York, NY 10011
(212) 741-3384

Brochures available.

Imports the latest in postmodern European furniture.

Bon Marché
55 W. 13th St.
New York, NY 10011
(212) 620-5550

Retailer of contemporary knock-down furniture and accessories.

Brayton International Collection
255 Swathmore Ave.
P.O. Box 7288
High Point, NC 27264
(919) 434-4151

Manufactures luxurious contemporary furnishings.

Brueton Industries Inc.
227-02 145th Rd.
Springfield Gardens, NY 11413
(718) 527-3000

Offers a broad selection of modern furniture classics.

C

Steven Caldwell
5721 16th N.E.
Seattle, WA 98105
(206) 525-4089

Makes handcrafted furniture; specializes in custom work.

Castelli Furniture, Inc.
116 Wilbur Pl.
P.O. Box 509
Bohemia, NY 11716
(516) 589-0707

Brochures available.

Specialists in seating for offices and institutions.

Charrette
31 Olympia Ave.
Woburn, MA 01888
(617) 935-6000

Catalogue available.

Supplies an extensive collection of office furniture and equipment.

The Children's Room
318 E. 45th St.
New York, NY 10017
(212) 687-3868

Catalogue available.

An expertly chosen collection of children's furnishings, available at its retail outlet or by mail.

C I Designs
574 Boston Ave.
P.O. Box 191
Medford, MA 02155
(617) 391-7800

Brochures available.

Offers a wide range of contemporary furniture and accessories.

Clairson International
720 S.W. 17th St.
Ocala, FL 32674
(904) 732-8734 or (800) 874-0007

Brochures available.

Veterans in the manufacture and sale of adjustable closet systems.

Closet Systems Corp.
1175 Broadway
Hewlett, NY 11557
(516) 569-1400

Brochures available.

Makers of the "Swinger System" and other closet organizers.

Conran's Mail Order
4 S. Middlesex Ave.
Cranbury, NJ 08512
(609) 655-4505

Catalogue, $2.

Innovative designs in home furnishings and accessories available by mail or at retail outlets in New York, Massachusetts, New Jersey, Pennsylvania, Washington, D.C., Virginia, and Maryland.

D

Peter Danko & Associates
7492F Old Alexander Ferry Rd.
Clinton, MD 20735
(301) 292-1653 or (800) 882-5300

Brochures available.

Creates sleek, handsome designs in contemporary furniture.

Door Store
3140 M Street N.W.
Washington, D.C. 10007
(202) 333-8170

Brochures available.

Modern furniture and accessories

for home and office, available at retail outlets in New York, Maryland, Virginia, Washington, D.C., Texas, Florida, California, and Pennsylvania. (Stores in California and Pennsylvania are called Homeplace.)

Dorfile Shelving Systems
P.O. Box 18937
Memphis, TN 38181
(901) 365-0479

Brochures available.

Manufactures a number of ingenious closet and shelving systems.

Dux Interiors Inc.
305 E. 63rd St.
New York, NY 10021
(212) 752-3897

Catalogue available.

Sophisticated contemporary furniture and fabrics imported from Sweden.

E

Curtis Erpelding
110 Union, #300
Seattle, WA 98101
(206) 625-0754

A craftsman who specializes in fine wood furniture; makes drawings and estimates available upon request.

F

Fifty/50
793 Broadway
New York, NY 10003
(212) 777-3208

Specialists in mid-century furniture and decorative arts.

Furniture of the Twentieth Century
227 W. 17th St.
New York, NY 10011
(212) 929-6023

Offers classic styles in modern and postmodern furniture.

G

General Mica Corp.
1850 N.E. 144 St.
N. Miami FL 33181
(305) 949-7247 or (305) 576-1268

Manufactures acrylic and laminated furniture in a variety of styles.

Greenbaum Collection
101 Washington St.
Paterson, NJ 07505
(201) 279-3000

Brochures available.

Imports luxurious, innovative contemporary furniture.

H

Hagerwood
1545 Marquette, S.W.
P.O. Box 9465
Grand Rapids, MI 49509
(616) 399-9151

Brochure available.

Manufacturer of handsome modular shelving systems.

Henredon Furniture Industries, Inc.
P.O. Box 70
Morganton, NC 28655
(704) 437-5261

Catalogues available.
Manufactures a wide range of modern furnishings for homes and offices.

Homeplace. *See* Door Store.

H.U.D.D.L.E.
3416 Wesley St.
Culver City, CA 90230
(213) 836-8001

Brochures available.

Designs and distributes avant-garde furniture and accessories.

I

Ikea
Plymouth Meeting Mall
Plymouth Meeting, PA 19462
(215) 834-0150

Catalogue available at stores in Pennsylvania and Virginia and by mail at outlets in Vancouver, B.C.; Edmonton, Alberta; Toronto, Ontario; Quebec City, Quebec; and Dartmouth, Nova Scotia.

Attractive, reasonably priced home furnishings and accessories imported from Europe.

Interna Designs
The Merchandise Mart, #6-168
Chicago, IL 60654
(312) 467-6076 or (800) 468-3762

Brochures available.

Importers of stylish European furniture.

International Contract Furnishings
305 E. 63rd St.
New York, NY 10021
(212) 750-0900

Brochures available.

Suppliers of sophisticated modern furniture; the latest in avant-garde designs.

Intrends International
P.O. Box 241
Scarsdale, NY 10583
(914) 472-5666

Catalogue available.

Offers a number of handsome folding and stacking chairs and modular wall units.

K

Vladimir Kagan Designs Inc.
232 E. 59th St.
New York, NY 10022
(212) 371-1512

Purveyor of exclusive luxury furniture and accessories.

King Refrigerator Corp.
7602 Woodhaven Blvd.
Glendale, NY 11385
(718) 897-2200

Catalogue available.

Manufactures compact kitchen units and refrigeration equipment

Peter Korn
4101 Lauriston St.
Philadelphia, Pa 19128
(215) 487-3287

Crafts fine wood furniture; custom orders are a specialty.

Robert Krups NA
7 Pearl Ct.
Allendale, NJ 07401
(201) 825-1116

Catalogue available.

North American outlet for Germany's largest manufacturer of small appliances.

L

Liza Lamb
122 Haller Blvd.
Ithaca, NY 14850
(607) 273-6790

Makes one-of-a-kind furniture designs using her own textiles.

The Fran Laufer Collection
New York Design Center
200 Lexington Ave., #1006
New York, NY 10016
(212) 686-7373

Imports contemporary Oriental furnishings and accessories.

Tom Loeser
80 Chestnut St.
Cambridge, MA 02139
(617) 661-9836 or (617) 868-5211

An artisan who specializes in sculptural furniture designs in fine wood.

Lübke International Design
P.O. Box 4795
High Point, NC 27263
(919) 884-8042

In Canada:

c/o Pieter Schat
299 Glenlake Ave.
P.O. Box 202, Stn. M
Toronto, Ont. M6S 4T3
(416) 769-0812

Brochures available.

Imports fine modern furniture from its factories in West Germany.

Lynk Inc.
8241 Melrose Dr.
Shawnee Mission, KS 66214
(913) 492-9202

Brochures available.

Imports and manufactures closet systems and wall storage units.

M

Magic Chef, Inc.
740 King Edward Ave., SE
Cleveland, TN 37311
(605) 472-3371

Brochures available.

Manufactures a broad selection of gas and electric appliances.

MDI
P.O. Box 19188
Washington, DC 20036

Imports contemporary European furnishings.

Modern Mode Inc.
111 San Leandro Blvd.
San Leandro, CA 94577
(415) 568-6650

Manufactures a comprehensive selection of contemporary furniture.

Molla Inc.
110 State St.
P.O. Box 797
Westbury, NY 11590
(212) 696-9211

Catalogues available.

Makes and distributes durable, good-looking outdoor furniture in a wide range of styles.

Murphy Door Bed Company, Inc.
40 E. 34th St.
New York, NY 10016

Brochures available.

Maker and distributor of the classic Murphy fold-down bed.

Museum of Modern Art
Publication Sales and Service
11 W. 53rd St.
New York, NY 10019
(212) 708-9400

Catalogue, $2.

Selections from the best designs in this world-renowned museum's permanent collection are chosen to be reproduced for sale in the retail shop and are available by mail.

N

Nienkämper
415 Finchdene Sq.
Scarborough, Ont. M1X 1B7
Canada
(416) 362-3434

In New York:

295 Madison Ave., #830
New York, NY 10017
(212) 661-4676

Brochures available.

Offers superbly designed contemporary furniture.

Norix Group Inc.
P.O. Box 298
Batavia, IL 60510
(312) 879-6160

Importers of striking contemporary furniture for both indoor and outdoor use.

O

Origlia USA Inc.
200 Lexington Ave.
New York, NY 10016
(212) 532-0075

Brochures available.

Imports unusual postmodern Italian furnishings and accessories.

P

Palazzetti Inc.
215 Lexington Ave.
New York, NY 10016
(212) 684-1199

Imports 20th-century furniture and accessories that are classics of modern design.

The Pine Factory Ltd.
1262 Plymouth Meeting Mall
Plymouth Meeting, PA 19462
(215) 825-7713

Brochures available.

Manufactures and distributes casual solid-pine furniture.

Placewares
351 Congress St.
Boston, MA 02210
(617) 451-2074

Catalogue, $2.

Specialists in portable furniture and accessories designed to make the most of available living space.

Plexability
200 Lexington Ave., #506
New York, NY 10016
(212) 679-7826

Deals exclusively in custom-made acrylic furniture and accessories.

Plexi-Craft Quality Products Corporation
514 W. 24th St.
New York, NY 10011
(212) 924-3244

Catalogue, $2.

Offers a wide range of Lucite and Plexiglas furniture.

The Pottery Barn, Inc.
175 Clearbrook Rd.
Elmsford, NY 10523
(914) 592-2330

Has several dozen retail outlets offering well-designed, reasonably priced contemporary furnishings.

Q

Quaker Industries
90 McMillen Rd.
Antioch, IL 60002
(312) 395-3300

Brochures available.

Manufactures closet and storage systems and a good selection of folding tables for both indoor and outdoor use.

R

Rangine Corporation
114 Union St.
P.O. Box 128
Millis, MA 02054
(617) 376-4545

Catalogue available.

Makes ingenious modular hanging and freestanding storage systems.

S

Scandinavian Design/ Scandinavian Gallery
Corporate Headquarters
Natick, MA 01760
(617) 655-2830 or (800) 225-4652

Specializes in imported and domestic teak and rosewood furnishings, offered at 64 stores throughout New England, the Mid-Atlantic states, and Hawaii. (New England stores are called Scandinavian Design; those in other areas, Scandinavian Gallery.)

Schulte Corp.
11450 Grooms Rd.
Cincinnati, OH 45242
(512) 489-9300

Brochures available.

Manufactures steel-wire closet and shelving systems to solve a variety of storage problems.

Sears Roebuck and Co.
Sears Tower
Chicago, IL 60684
(312) 875-2500

An extensive line of home furnishings available by mail order and at retail outlets throughout the United States.

Shoji Workshop
21-10 31st Ave.
Astoria, NY 11106
(718) 274-9351

Brochure available.

Manufactures and installs classic Japanese shoji screens.

Sico Incorporated
7525 Cahill Rd.
P.O. Box 1169
Minneapolis, MN 55440
(612) 941-1700

Brochure available.

Makes space-saving, attractive fold-down beds and storage units.

René Soulard
1833 13th Ave., #208
Seattle, WA 98122
(206) 328-1164

An artist who creates one-of-a-kind furniture designs in wood.

Speed Queen Company
Shepard St.
P.O. Box 990
Ripon, WI 54971
(414) 748-3121

Brochures available.

Manufactures and distributes an extensive line of major appliances.

StackAShelf Ltd.
160 Columbia Ave. W.
P.O. Box 10
Waterloo, Ont. N2J 3Z6
Canada
(519) 884-6400

Brochures available.

Makes closet systems and companion knock-down storage pieces.

Stay-Neat Closet Interiors
21 Pine St.
P.O. Box 219
Rockaway, NJ 07866
(201) 263-0270

Brochures available.

Specializes in closet systems and accessories.

Stendig International, Inc.
410 E. 62nd St.
New York, NY 10021
(212) 838-6050

Brochures available.

Imports a wide range of contemporary furniture; manufactures its own line of fine textiles.

Strictly Country
P.O. Box 6069
New Philadelphia, OH 44663
(216) 343-7536

Catalogue, $2.

Specializes in informal furniture and accessories.

T

Thayer Coggin Inc.
P.O. Box 5867
High Point, NC 27262
(919) 889-1700

Brochures available.

Manufactures quality furniture and accessories for home and office.

Thonet
491 E. Princess St.
P.O. Box 1587
York, PA 17405

Brochures available.

Manufactures a large selection of contemporary home and office furnishings.

Tromploy
400 Lafayette St.
New York, NY 10003
(212) 420-1639

A group of artists who are wizards at creating visual foolery on canvas or on furniture.

V

Van Pelt/Siesel
845 3rd Ave.
New York, NY 10022
(212) 759-6500

Manufactures ready-to-assemble modular wall systems in various styles and finishes.

W

Tom Wessells
4 Graham Dr.
Newport News, VA 23606
(804) 599-5615

An artisan who creates fine hand-crafted wood furniture.

Westnofa USA Inc.
7040 N. Austin Ave.
Niles, IL 60648
(312) 647-7415

Brochures available.

Imports revolutionary designs in home furnishings from its parent company in Scandinavia.

Whirlpool Corporation.
Benton Harbor, MI 49022
(616) 926-5000

Manufactures both large and small appliances for the home.

Workbench
470 Park Ave. S.
New York, NY 10016
(212) 532-7900

Brochures available.

Has more than 60 stores spread across the United States; each offers a broad selection of contemporary home furnishings and accessories.

Rick Wrigley
80 Race St.
Holyoke, MA 01040
(413) 536-2034

A talented cabinetmaker who designs and creates fine wood furniture.

Bibliography

Almeida, Philip. *How to Decorate a Dump.* Secaucus, N.J.: Lyle Stuart Inc., 1983.

Bradford, Barbara Taylor. *Making Space Grow.* New York: Simon & Schuster, 1979.

Cobb, Hubbard H. *The Dream House Encyclopedia.* New York: Peter H. Wyden, Inc., 1970.

Conran, Terence. *The Bed and Bath Book.* New York: Crown Publishers Inc., 1978.

_____. *The Kitchen Book.* New York: Crown Publishers Inc., 1977.

_____. *The New House Book.* New York: Villard Books, 1985.

Editors of Apartment Life Magazine. *The New Apartment Book.* New York: Harmony Books, 1983. (Revised text by Cara Greenberg).

Faulkner, Sarah. *Planning a Home: A Practical Guide to Interior Design.* New York: Holt, Rinehart & Winston, 1979.

Gilliatt, Mary. *Decorating: A Realistic Guide.* New York: Pantheon Books, 1977.

Grow, Lawrence. *Modern Style: A Catalogue of Contemporary Design.* Pittstown, N.J.: The Main Street Press, 1985.

Knox, Gerald M., Ed. *Stretching Living Space.* Des Moines: Meredith Corporation, 1983.

Kron, Joan. *Home-Psych: The Social Psychology of Home and Decoration.* New York: Clarkson N. Potter, Inc., 1983.

Kron, Joan and Suzanne Slesin. *High-Tech: The Industrial Style and Source Book for the Home.* New York: Clarkson N. Potter, Inc., 1978.

Leman, Ellen. *The Spacemaker Book.* New York: The Viking Press, 1977.

Naar, Jon. *Your Space: How to Put It Together for Practically Nothing.* New York: St. Martin's Press, 1979.

Prowler, Donald. *Modest Mansions: Design Ideas for Luxurious Living.* Emmaus, Pa: Rodale Press, 1985.

Schneider, Tom. *The Moveable Nest.* New York: Dell Publishing Co. Inc., 1981.

Slesin, Suzanne. *The New York Times Home Book of Modern Design Styles, Problems, and Solutions.* New York: Times Books, 1982.

U.S. Bureau of the Census. *Statistical Abstract of the United States*, 106th Edition. Washington, D.C.: 1985.

Index

Aalto, Alvo, 16, 49, 50
Akko Inc., 19, 35, 41, 52, 175
Allibert, 156, 157, 158, 159
Alumaloy. *See* Molla.
Alumax Corp., 114, 127, 141
Amisco Industries, 43, 61, 66, 74, 140, 145
Anselmi, Anna, 18, 36
Appliances, 166-169
Arconas Corp., 27, 30, 78
ARD Custom Kitchens and Baths, 169
Artek, 50
Artemide, Inc., 34, 43, 155
Atelier International Ltd., 48
Axiom Designs, 75

Baskets, 123, 177
Baughman, Milo, 68
Bedcraft, 65
Beds, 55-68: bunk, 134, 135, 137, 139, 140; children's, 134-140; convertible, 58-60, 67, 68; fold-down/folding, 62-64; futons, 57, 65, 66; platform, 65; trundle, 61, 135, 136, 139
Belotti, Giandomenico, 22, 49
Benches, 41, 79-80, 175
Berkowicz, Michael Zevy, 38, 42, 52, 173
Better Houseware Corp., 122, 128, 170
Bicycles, exercise, 176
Bieffe U.S.A., 18, 22, 23, 28, 36, 50, 104
Blanket racks, 175
Bon Marché, 61, 85, 176

Bookcases/shelves, 97, 100, 102, 104, 105, 106, 107, 109
Brayton International Collection, 72
Breuer, Marcel, 13, 16
Brueton Industries Inc., 77
Brunati of Italy, 75
Busnelli of Italy, 74

Cabinets, 93-110: children's, 136, 137, 138, 140, 142, 143; file, 85-88, 91, 109-110; hanging, 109-110; modular, 96-103, 106-110
Caldwell, Steven, 80
Canisters, 129
Carter, Ronald, 41, 48
Castelli Furniture, Inc., 29, 35, 76
Castiglione, Achille, 36
Chairs, 11-30: children's, 141-143; folding, 14-19, 35, 38, 150, 151, 153, 156; lounge, 30, 157; outdoor, 150-157; stacking, 20-29, 34, 49, 150, 152, 154, 155, 157
Charrette, 87, 90, 92
Cherner, Norman, 20, 23
Children's furnishings, 134-146: beds, 134-140; bunks, 135, 137; desks, 137, 142, 143, 146; seating, 141, 142, 143; storage, 141-144, 146
Children's Room, The, 135, 138, 142, 143
C I Designs, 18, 75, 153
Clairson International, 116, 120, 129
Closet Maid. *See* Clairson International.
Closet systems, 114-119
Closet Systems Corp., 117

Coathangers/coat racks, 174-175
Columbo, Joe, 92
Conran, Terence, 107
Conran's, 66, 86, 96, 106, 107, 119, 122, 136, 137, 153
Creamer, Catherine, 173

Danko, Peter & Associates, 15, 21, 65
Decking, 153
DePas, D'Urbino, Lomazzi, 77
Desks, 84-88: folding, 84, 85; knockdown, 86, 87; modular, 86, 87, 88
Dish racks, 170, 171
Door Store, 65, 73, 84, 89, 92, 100, 137, 144, 150, 151, 171
Dorfile Shelving Systems, 115, 127, 129
Dux Interiors, Inc., 58, 62
Dysthe, Sven Ivar, 24

Eames, Charles, 173
Eichenberger, Hans, 39
Elberfeld, Hartmut, 24
Elfa System. *See* Lynk and Placewares.
Erpelding, Curtis, 29, 104, 105, 174

Fans, 169, 176
Fifty/50, 20, 173
File cabinets. *See* Cabinets
Friedman, Sally, 177
Friedman, Stanley Jay, 77
FRZ-Mettallwarenfabrik, 49

Furniture of the Twentieth Century, 18, 20, 23, 28, 36
Futons. *See* Beds.

Gammelgaard, Niels, 39
General Mica Corp., 44, 51
Glastonbury, Abbott of, 12
Gray, Eileen, 46, 49
Greenbaum Collection, 44, 74
Grimsrud, Tone, 30

Hagberg, Knut and Marianne, 139
Hagerwood, 97
Haigh Space, 22
Hansen, Roald Steen, 174
Heaters, 169
Henredon Furniture Industries, Inc., 53
High chairs, 145
Hille International, 27
Home-Psych, 7
Homeplace. *See* Door Store.
H.U.D.D.L.E., 134
Hull Urban Design Development Laboratory, Etcetera. *See* H.U.D.D.L.E.

Ikea, 39, 47, 54, 60, 79, 90, 100, 101, 139, 144, 145
Interna Designs, 17, 27, 41, 48
International Contract Furnishings, 22, 77
Intrends International, 38

Jelinek, Tomas, 54

Kagan, Vladimir, Designs Inc., 45
Kandinsky, Wassily, 16
Kartell, 162
King Refrigerator Corp., 164, 168
Kinsman, Rodney, 23, 104
Kirkpatrick, Michael, 18
Knoll, Michael, 72
Korn, Peter, 80
Kotzian, Henry, 44
Kron, Joan, 7
Krups, Robert, NA, 169

Lamb, Liza, 42
Lamb, Thomas, 29

Laufer Collection, The Fran, 172, 177
Le Corbusier, 16
Lepoix, Louis Lucien, 49
Loeser, Tom, 15, 36
Lounge chairs. *See* Chairs.
Lübke International Design, 24
Lyndon, Maynard Hale and Lu Wendel, 103
LyndonDesign, 38
Lynk Inc., 53, 88, 124

Mackintosh, Charles Rennie, 48
Magazine racks, 110
Magic Chef, Inc., 166, 167, 169
Magistretti, Vico, 34, 43, 49, 155
Mallet-Stevens, Robert, 20
MDI, 23
Memphis Group, 28
Mengshoel, H.C., 17
Miles, Peter, Furniture, 41, 48
Miller, Rick, 65
Modern Mode Inc., 23
Molla Inc., 152, 162
Mourgue, Olivier, 30
Murphy Door Bed Company, Inc., 63
Murphy, William, 63
Museum of Modern Art, 16, 30, 35, 39, 46, 49, 50, 174

Nienkämper, 29
Nilsen, Torstein, 14
Norix Group Inc., 154

Opsvik, Peter, 17, 141
Origlia USA Inc., 107, 175, 177
Outdoor furniture, 147-162: chairs, 150-157; tables, 158-162; trolleys, 158, 161, 162

Paintings, 177
Palazzetti Inc., 16, 20, 46, 50
Pierantonio Bonacina of Italy, 23
Pine Factory, Ltd., The, 59, 96, 103, 136
Piretti, Giancarlo, 35
Piva, Paolo, 74
Placewares, 38, 53, 72, 86, 88, 91, 96, 102, 103, 121, 123, 124, 125, 127, 129, 146, 162, 171
Plexability, 38, 42, 53, 173
Plexi-Craft Quality Products Corp., 54, 110

Poltrona Frau, 17
Pottery Barn, Inc., The, 15, 37, 45, 66, 105, 151

Quaker Industries, 35, 120, 121, 130, 160, 161

Rangine Corporation, 109, 110
Relling, Ingmar, 19
Rovel. *See* Better Houseware Corp.
Rowland, David, 26

Sapper, Richard, 49
Scandinavian Design/Scandinavian Gallery, 46, 50, 59, 97
Schulte Corp., 115, 126, 146
Screens, folding, 172-173
Sears Roebuck and Co., 176
Sebel, 154
Shelving, 93-110: children's, 141-144, 146; for clothes closets, 114-117; freestanding, 96-108; hanging, 109-110; utility, 120-130
Shoe racks, 116
Shoji Workshop, The, 172
Sico Incorporated, 64
Snodgrass, Warren, 25
Sofas, 69-80: convertible, 58-60; daybeds, 72, 74, 75; knockdown 73; love seats, 72, 73, 74, 75; sectional/modular, 76-78
Sorensen, Johnny, 26
Sottsass Associates, 28, 50
Sottsass, Ettore, 28, 49
Soulard, René, 40
Speed Queen Company, 166
StackAShelf Ltd., 108, 114
Stay-Neat Closet Interiors, 117
Stendig International Inc., 39, 74
Stepladders, 176
Stools, 14, 141, 142, 145
Storage, 111-130: baskets, 123, 177; children's, 141-144, 146; closet systems, 114-119; freestanding/modular, 120-124; hanging, 125-130; trolleys, 122; utility, 120-130
Strictly Country, 47, 80

Tables, 31-54: computer, 51, 89, 109; drafting, 90-92, 109; extension/expansion, 44-48; folding, 34-38, 158-162; knockdown, 34, 36, 38; legs for, 177, on casters, 49-54, 158, 161, 162; outdoor, 34, 158-162; stacking/nesting, 39-43
Tea carts. *See* Trolleys.
Thayer Coggin Inc., 68, 78
Thonet, 25, 26, 64, 67, 118, 125
Thygesen, Rud, 26
Towel racks, 169, 170, 171
Trolleys, 49-54, 122, 123, 158, 161, 162
Tromploy, 177

Trundle beds. *See* Beds.
Tysnes, Olav Rolv, 25

Valets, 175
Van der Rohe, Mies, 16
Van Pelt/Siesel, 51, 98, 99
Vitamaster, 176
Vogtherr, Burkhard, 72

Wardrobes, 118-119, 138
Wessells, Tom, 79, 102

Westnofa USA Inc., 14, 17, 19, 24, 25, 30, 141
Whirlpool Corporation, 166, 167
Workbench, 61, 88, 91, 99
World Pictures, 174
Wrigley, Rick, 173

Xylem, 40

Zanotta of Italy, 36